A Matter of Interpretation

☆

A Matter of Interpretation

☆

FEDERAL COURTS AND THE LAW

☆

AN ESSAY BY
ANTONIN SCALIA

WITH COMMENTARY BY
AMY GUTMANN, EDITOR
GORDON S. WOOD
LAURENCE H. TRIBE
MARY ANN GLENDON
RONALD DWORKIN

PRINCETON UNIVERSITY PRESS

PRINCETON, NEW JERSEY

Library of Congress Cataloging-in-Publication Data

Scalia, Antonin.
A matter of interpretation : federal courts and the law:
an essay / by Antonin Scalia ; with commentary
by Amy Gutmann, editor . . . [et al.].
p. cm. — (The University Center for Human Values series)
Includes bibliographical references and index.
ISBN 0-691-02630-0
ISBN 0-691-00400-5 (pbk.)
1. United States—Constitutional law—Interpretation and
construction. 2. Judge-made law—United States.
3. Law—United States—Interpretation and construction.
I. Gutmann, Amy. II. Title. III. Series.
KF4552.S28 1997
347.73'2634—dc20
[347.3073534] 96-40969 CIP

This book has been composed in Palatino

Sixth printing, and first paperback printing, 1998

http://pup.princeton.edu

Printed in the United States of America

13 15 17 19 20 18 16 14 12

ISBN-13: 978-0-691-00400-6

ISBN-10: 0-691-00400-5

☆ *Contents* ☆

☆ *Preface* ☆

THE RULE OF LAW is essential to constitutional democracy. But its implications for how judges should interpret the law are complex and contested, as evidenced by Justice Antonin Scalia's elegant essay and the respectful but challenging responses to it by Professors Ronald Dworkin, Mary Ann Glendon, Laurence Tribe, and Gordon Wood. Together these eminent legal minds address one of the most important legal questions of our time: How should judges interpret statutory and constitutional law so that its rule is a reality that is consistent with a constitutional democratic ideal?

Should the aim of judges be to determine the intent of the legislators who made the law? On its face, this appears to be a democratic aim: to capture the intention of the law's makers, legislators who are accountable to the majority. Justice Scalia offers a powerful critique of this popular idea that judicial interpretation should be guided by legislative intent. A government of laws, not of men, means that the *unexpressed* intent of legislators must not bind citizens. Laws mean what they actually say, not what legislators intended them to say but did not write into the law's text for anyone (and everyone so moved) to read. This is the essence of the philosophy of law that Justice Scalia develops here in more detail. The philosophy is called textualism, or originalism, since it is the *original* meaning of the text—applied to present circumstances—that should govern judicial interpretation of statutes and the Constitution.

The idea that the law is what the words that constitute it mean is of course too simple. Most words are open to multiple interpretations. To say that laws are what their words mean would be to leave the meaning of most laws unacceptably ambiguous. The complexity of figuring out what laws mean should not prevent us—as it does not prevent Justice Scalia—from eliminating indefensible responses to the challenge of interpreting

vii

apparently ambiguous laws. Justice Scalia criticizes two alternatives to textualism—judicial decision making according to subjective intent and judicial creation of a "living" or "evolving"
Constitution—as indefensible ways of interpreting (or failing to
interpret) the law. But he also goes well beyond criticism; he develops and defends the merits of his philosophy of textualism.

Justice Scalia shows that textualism is not wooden, unimaginative, or pedestrian; least of all is it boring. Textualism is not
strict constructivism, although (he says) strict constructivism
would be better than nontextualism. "Words do have a limited
range of meaning, and no interpretation that goes beyond that
range is permissible." Scalia's respondents take up his challenge: to show what could possibly be wrong with the commonsensical view that judicial interpretation should be guided by
the text and not by intentions or ideals external to it, and by the
original meaning of the text, not by its evolving meaning over
time.

The questions raised by Justice Scalia's commentators are of
two kinds: What do judges committed to textualism do when
the text is ambiguous? More critically: Why should judges desist
from invoking moral principles and other nontextual aids to
help interpret the law when the text itself is an inadequate
guide?

Justice Scalia anticipates both challenges in his essay, and he
also replies to them in his "Response." Judges must do their best
to figure out, first, the original meaning of laws and, second, the
practical implications given new contexts for those original
meanings. In most cases, judges will be successful in so doing.
"Originalism" helps specify "textualism" and helps judges ar-
rive at definite interpretations of the text even when the words
are ambiguous. "There is plenty of room for disagreement as to
what original meaning was, and even more as to how that original meaning applies to the situation before the court," Justice
Scalia writes. "But the originalist at least knows what he is looking for: the original meaning of the text. Often—indeed, I dare

say usually—that is easy to discern and simple to apply. Sometimes (though not very often) there will be disagreement regarding the original meaning; and sometimes there will be disagreement as to how that original meaning applies to new and
unforeseen phenomena."

But the disagreement of views about interpreting the law represented in this volume ranges much further than resolving ambiguity about original meaning or uncertainty about how to
apply original meaning to new and unforeseen phenomena.
Professors Wood, Tribe, Glendon, and Dworkin also take issue
with other claims that Justice Scalia makes on behalf of textualism. They question whether textualism, as Justice Scalia under-
stands it, is the legal philosophy that is most defensible or most
consistent with democratic values. All the commentators concur
with Justice Scalia's critique of interpreting the law according
to either subjective legislative intent or a judge's favorite moral
philosophy. But they suggest other alternatives—including
some significantly different versions of textualism—that are apparently defensible and democratic, even if not definitive, op-
tions. They argue that these alternatives do not suffer from the
same devastating flaws as the interpretative strategies that Justice Scalia criticizes.

Professor Wood joins Justice Scalia in worrying about the tension between judicial lawmaking and democracy. Judges, he
agrees, should be interpreters, not makers of the law. But Professor Wood, whose area of expertise is American history, also
worries that Justice Scalia underestimates the degree to which
judicial lawmaking is part of the very constitution of American
democracy, albeit an extremely controversial part. Thomas Jefferson struggled, unsuccessfully, to end "the eccentric impulses
of whimsical, capricious designing man" and to make the judge
"a mere machine." But not all, or even most, of the founding
fathers shared Jefferson's aims. Nor did the design of the judiciary follow Jefferson's plan. According to Professor Wood: "The
courts became independent entities whose relationship with the

sovereign people made them appear to have nearly equal authority with the legislatures in the creation of law. The transformation was monumental." If Professor Wood's interpretation of American history is correct, then the blurring of legislative and judicial matters may be the rule rather than the exception for postcolonial America.

Professor Tribe defends a version of textualism that helps explain why this blurring may be necessary. He doubts that judges, historians, or anyone else can discover enough about the law to render decisions in many cases by interpreting the text only in the way that Justice Scalia recommends. Yet Professor Tribe also wants to prevent judges from legislating their personal preferences or values under the guise of constitutional interpretation. To prevent judges from usurping democratic authority, he suggests a strategy quite different from Justice Scalia's. "[O]ne must concede," Professor Tribe says, "how difficult the task [of constitutional interpretation] is; avoid all pretense that it can be reduced to a passive process of *discovering* rather than *constructing* an interpretation; and replace such pretense with a forthright account, incomplete and inconclusive though it might be, of why one deems his or her proposed construction of the text to be worthy of acceptance, in light of the Constitution as a whole and the history of its interpretation."

Professor Tribe therefore takes up Justice Scalia's challenge by doubting "that any defensible set of ultimate 'rules' [of interpretation] exists. Insights and perspectives, yes; rules no." Judges can still know how *not* to interpret laws, but they "must of necessity look outside the Constitution itself" for guidance, as must all who are authorized by the Constitution to interpret it and duty-bound to adhere to its provisions. The "Constitution's written text has primacy and must be deemed the ultimate point of departure," and "nothing irreconcilable with the text can properly be considered part of the Constitution." Nonetheless, "[t]here is . . . nothing in the text itself that proclaims the Constitution's text to be the sole or ultimate point of reference—and, even if there were, such a self-referential proclamation would raise the problem of infinite regress and would, in addition, leave unanswered the very question with which we began: how is the text's *meaning* to be ascertained?"

Professor Glendon focuses on a neglected topic, raised by Justice Scalia's critique of extending common-law habits to statutory and constitutional law: the merits of common-law habits, applied to the realm of the common law. "Many of our interpretive ills are due to the survival of common-law habits in the world of enacted law," Professor Glendon writes, "But it ought to be said that those habits were good ones, even if ill-adapted to statutory and constitutional interpretation. It is cause for concern, therefore, that they seem to be deteriorating." *Stare decisis*, by protecting the power of precedent, lends stability to the expectations of citizens. There could be far worse, Professor Glendon suggests, than a Supreme Court that followed common-law methods "in the sense of attending in each case to providing a fair resolution of the case at hand, mooring that decision in text and tradition, fairly exposing its reasoning processes, and providing guidance to parties in future cases." By contrast, Professor Glendon asks us to consider a Court whose "rulings look less like the reasoned elaboration of principle than like the products of majority vote. At times the Court appears just to be lurching along in irrational and unpredictable fashion, like the monster in the old version of *Frankenstein*." This kind of Court would give us far more to fear, Glendon vividly argues, than one that followed common-law patterns of principled building upon precedent.

Professor Dworkin defends a different version of originalism from Justice Scalia's. The idea that distinguishes Professor Dworkin's version from that of Justice Scalia is that "key constitutional provisions, as a matter of their original meaning, set out abstract principles rather than concrete or dated rules. If so, then the application of these abstract principles to particular cases, which takes fresh judgment, must be continually reviewed, not in an attempt to find substitutes for what the Constitution says, but out of respect for what it says." Professor Dworkin argues that this interpretative strategy is both true to the text and principled. "[W]hy," he asks, "shouldn't the 'framers' have thought that a combination of concrete and abstract rights would best secure the (evidently abstract) goals they set out in the preamble?" Why shouldn't we think that wise statesmen would realize that their views were not the last word on the subject? Moreover, Professor Dworkin argues, "There *was* no generally accepted understanding of the right of free speech on which the framers could have based a dated clause even if they had wanted to write one." When the debate raged over the Sedition Act of 1798, "[n]o one supposed that the First Amendment codified some current and settled understanding, and the deep division among them showed that there was no settled understanding to codify."

The division among the contributors to this book may not be as deep as that between the authors of the Sedition Act and their critics, but there is certainly no settled answer among them to the question of how judges should interpret statutory and constitutional law. Although it is up to each reader to adjudicate this disagreement, Justice Scalia's respectful yet spirited response to his commentators will undoubtedly increase our understanding of the merits of alternative answers and heighten our awareness of the stakes for all American citizens.

This book originated in an invitation by the University Center for Human Values at Princeton University to Justice Scalia to deliver the Tanner Lectures, and to Professors Dworkin, Glendon, Tribe, and Wood to offer commentaries on them. We are all thankful to the Tanner Trust for their generous support of the Tanner Lectures and to the University Center for Human Values for hosting the lectures each year. We are especially grateful to Mrs. Grace Adams Tanner and the late Mr. Obert Clark Tanner for endowing the Tanner Lectures and to Mr. Laurance S. Rockefeller for endowing the University Center for Human Values. As part of the University Center for Human Values publication series, this book conveys our mutual dedication to giving voice to perspectives that challenge conventional ways of thinking and thereby contribute to our reflecting more deeply and broadly about issues of great human significance.

AMY GUTMANN

Laurance S. Rockefeller University Professor
University Center for Human Values
Princeton University

A Matter of Interpretation

☆

Common-Law Courts in a Civil-Law System: The Role of United States Federal Courts in Interpreting the Constitution and Laws

☆

ANTONIN SCALIA

THE FOLLOWING essay attempts to explain the current neglected state of the science of construing legal texts, and offers a few suggestions for improvement. It is addressed not just to lawyers but to all thoughtful Americans who share our national obsession with the law.

THE COMMON LAW

The first year of law school makes an enormous impact upon the mind. Many students remark upon the phenomenon. They experience a sort of intellectual rebirth, the acquisition of a whole new mode of perceiving and thinking. Thereafter, even if they do not yet know much law, they do—as the expression goes—"think like a lawyer."

The overwhelming majority of the courses taught in that first year, and surely the ones that have the most profound effect, teach the substance, and the methodology, of the common law—torts, for example; contracts; property; criminal law.

I am grateful for technical and research assistance by Matthew P. Previn, and for substantive suggestions by Eugene Scalia.

American lawyers cut their teeth upon the common law. To understand what an effect that must have, you must appreciate that the common law is not really common law, except insofar as judges can be regarded as common. That is to say, it is not "customary law," or a reflection of the people's practices, but is rather law developed by the judges. Perhaps in the very infancy of Anglo-Saxon law it could have been thought that the courts were mere expositors of generally accepted social practices; and certainly, even in the full maturity of the common law, a well-established commercial or social practice could form the basis for a court's decision. But from an early time—as early as the Year Books, which record English judicial decisions from the end of the thirteenth century to the beginning of the sixteenth—any equivalence between custom and common law had ceased to exist, except in the sense that the doctrine of *stare decisis* rendered prior judicial decisions "custom." The issues coming before the courts involved, more and more, refined questions to which customary practice provided no answer.

Oliver Wendell Holmes's influential book *The Common Law*[1]— which is still suggested reading for entering law students—talks a little bit about Germanic and early English custom. But mostly it talks about individual court decisions, and about the judges, famous and obscure, who wrote them: Chief Justice Choke, Doderidge, J., Lord Holt, Redfield, C.J., Rolle, C.J., Hankford, J., Baron Parke, Lord Ellenborough, Peryam, C.B., Brett, J., Cockburn, C.J., Popham, C.J., Hyde, C.J., and on and on and on. Holmes's book is a paean to reason, and to the men who brought that faculty to bear in order to *create* Anglo-American law.

This is the image of the law—the common law—to which an aspiring American lawyer is first exposed, even if he has not read Holmes over the previous summer as he was supposed to. He learns the law, not by reading statutes that promulgate it or treatises that summarize it, but rather by studying the judicial opinions that invented it. This is the famous case-law method,

---

[1] Oliver Wendell Holmes, Jr., *The Common Law* (1881).

pioneered by Harvard Law School in the last century, and brought to movies and TV by the redoubtable Professor Kingsfield of *Love Story* and *The Paper Chase*. The student is directed to read a series of cases, set forth in a text called a "casebook," designed to show how the law developed. In the field of contracts, for example, he reads, and discusses in class, the famous old case of *Hadley* v. *Baxendale*,[2] decided a century and a half ago by the English Court of Exchequer: A mill in Gloucester ground to a halt (so to speak) because of a cracked crankshaft. To get a new one made, it was necessary to send the old one, as a model, to the manufacturer of the mill's steam engine, in Greenwich. The miller sent one of his workers to a carrier's office to see how long the delivery would take; the worker told the carrier's clerk that the mill was stopped, and that the shaft must be sent immediately. The clerk replied that if the shaft was received by noon, it would be delivered the next day. The miller presented the shaft to the carrier before noon the next day and paid the fee to have it transported; but because of the carrier's neglect it was delivered several days late, with the result that several additional days passed before the mill got back into service. The miller sought, as damages for breach of the shipping contract, his lost profits for those days, which were of course many times what the carrier had received as the shipping charge. The carrier said that he was not liable for such remote consequences.

Now this was a fairly subtle and refined point of law. As was the case with most legal points that became the subject of litigation, it could not really be said that there existed a general practice that the court could impose as common, customary law. The court decided, essentially, that the carrier was right, laying down the very important rule, that in a suit for breach of contract not *all* damages suffered because of the breach can be recovered, but only those that "could have been fairly and reasonably contemplated by both the parties when they made [the] contract." The opinion contains some policy reasons for that result, citation of a few earlier opinions by English courts, and

---

[2] 9 Ex. 341, 156 Eng. Rep. 145 (1854).

citation of not a single snippet of statutory law—though counsel arguing the case did bring to the court's attention the disposition set forth in the French Civil Code. For there *was* no relevant English statutory law; contract law was almost entirely the creation and domain of English judges.

I must interject at this point that even according to the new rule—that only reasonably foreseeable damages are recoverable—the miller rather than the carrier *should* have won the case. The court's opinion simply overlooks the fact that the carrier was *informed* that the mill was stopped; it must have been quite clear to the carrier's clerk that restarting the mill was the reason for the haste, and that profits would be lost while the mill was idle. But if you think it is terribly important that the case came out wrong, you miss the point of the common law. In the grand scheme of things, whether the right party won is really secondary. Famous old cases are famous, you see, not because they came out right, but because the rule of law they announced was the intelligent one. Common-law courts performed two functions: One was to apply the law to the facts. All adjudicators—French judges, arbitrators, even baseball umpires and football referees—do that. But the second function, and the more important one, was to *make* the law.

If you were sitting in on Professor Kingsfield's class when *Hadley* v. *Baxendale* was the assigned reading, you would find that the class discussion would not end with the mere description and dissection of the opinion. Various "hypotheticals" would be proposed by the crusty (yet, under it all, good-hearted) old professor, testing the validity and the sufficiency of the "foreseeability" rule. What if, for example, you are a blacksmith, and a young knight rides up on a horse that has thrown a shoe. He tells you he is returning to his ancestral estate, Blackacre, which he must reach that very evening to claim his inheritance, or else it will go to his wicked, no-good cousin, the sheriff of Nottingham. You contract to put on a new shoe, for the going rate of three farthings. The shoe is defective, or is badly shod, the horse goes lame, and the knight reaches Blackacre too late.

Are you really liable for the full amount of his inheritance? Is it reasonable to impose that degree of liability for three farthings? Would not the parties have set a different price if liability of that amount had been contemplated? Ought there not to be, in other words, some limiting principle to damages beyond mere foreseeability? Indeed, might not that principle—call it presumed assumption of risk—explain why *Hadley* v. *Baxendale* reached the right result after all, though not for the precise reason it assigned?

What intellectual fun all of this is! It explains why first-year law school is so exhilarating: because it consists of playing common-law judge, which in turn consists of playing king—devising, out of the brilliance of one's own mind, those laws that ought to govern mankind. How exciting! And no wonder so many law students, having drunk at this intoxicating well, aspire for the rest of their lives to be judges!

Besides the ability to think about, and devise, the "best" legal rule, there is another skill imparted in the first year of law school that is essential to the making of a good common-law judge. It is the technique of what is called "distinguishing" cases. That is a necessary skill, because an absolute prerequisite to common-law lawmaking is the doctrine of *stare decisis*—that is, the principle that a decision made in one case will be followed in the next. Quite obviously, without such a principle common-law courts would not be making any "law"; they would just be resolving the particular dispute before them. It is the requirement that future courts adhere to the principle underlying a judicial decision which causes that decision to be a legal rule. (There is no such requirement in the civil-law system, where it is the text of the law rather than any prior judicial interpretation of that text which is authoritative. Prior judicial opinions are consulted for their persuasive effect, much as academic commentary would be; but they are not *binding*.)

Within such a precedent-bound common-law system, it is critical for the lawyer, or the judge, to establish whether the case at hand falls within a principle that has already been decided.

7

Hence the technique—or the art, or the game—of "distinguishing" earlier cases. It is an art or a game, rather than a science, because what constitutes the "holding" of an earlier case is not well defined and can be adjusted to suit the occasion. At its broadest, the holding of a case can be said to be the analytical principle that produced the judgment—in *Hadley* v. *Baxendale*, for example, the principle that damages for breach of contract must be foreseeable. In the narrowest sense, however (and courts will squint narrowly when they wish to avoid an earlier decision), the holding of a case cannot go beyond the facts that were before the court. Assume, for example, that a painter contracts with me to paint my house green and paints it instead a god-awful puce. And assume that not I, but my *neighbor*, sues the painter for this breach of contract. The court would dismiss the suit on the ground that (in legal terminology) there was no "privity of contract": the contract was between the painter and *me*, not between the painter and my neighbor.[3] Assume, however, a later case in which a company contracts with me to repair my home computer; it does a bad job, and as a consequence my wife loses valuable files she has stored in the computer. *She* sues the computer company. Now the broad rationale of the earlier case (no suit will lie where there is no privity of contract) would dictate dismissal of this complaint as well. But a good common-law lawyer would argue, and some good common-law judges have held, that that rationale does not extend to this *new* fact situation, in which the breach of a contract relating to something used in the home harms a family member, though not the one who made the contract.[4] The earlier case, in other words, is "distinguishable."

It should be apparent that by reason of the doctrine of *stare decisis*, as limited by the principle I have just described, the common law grew in a peculiar fashion—rather like a Scrabble board. No rule of decision previously announced could be *erased*, but qualifications could be *added* to it. The first case lays

---

[3] *See, e.g.*, Monahan v. Town of Methuen, 558 N.E. 2d 951, 957 (Mass. 1990).

[4] *See, e.g.*, Grodstein v. McGivern, 154 A. 794 (Pa. 1931).

on the board: "No liability for breach of contractual duty without privity"; the next player adds "unless injured party is member of household." And the game continues.

As I have described, this system of making law by judicial opinion, and making law by distinguishing earlier cases, is what every American law student, every newborn American lawyer, first sees when he opens his eyes. And the impression remains for life. His image of the great judge—the Holmes, the Cardozo—is the man (or woman) who has the intelligence to discern the best rule of law for the case at hand and then the skill to perform the broken-field running through earlier cases that leaves him free to impose that rule: distinguishing one prior case on the left, straight-arming another one on the right, high-stepping away from another precedent about to tackle him from the rear, until (bravo!) he reaches the goal—good law. That image of the great judge remains with the former law student when he himself becomes a judge, and thus the common-law tradition is passed on.

DEMOCRATIC LEGISLATION

All of this would be an unqualified good, were it not for a trend in government that has developed in recent centuries, called democracy. In most countries, judges are no longer agents of the king, for there are no kings. In England, I suppose they can be regarded as in a sense agents of the legislature, since the Supreme Court of England is theoretically the House of Lords. That was once the system in the American colonies as well; the legislature of Massachusetts is still honorifically called the General Court of Massachusetts. But the highest body of Massachusetts judges is called the Supreme Judicial Court, because at about the time of the founding of our federal republic this country embraced the governmental principle of separation of powers.[5] That doctrine is praised, as the cornerstone of the

[5] *See* Plaut v. Spendthrift Farms, Inc., 115 S. Ct. 1447, 1453–56 (1995).

proposed federal Constitution, in *The Federalist* No. 47. Consider the compatibility of what Madison says in that number with the ancient system of lawmaking by judges. Madison quotes Montesquieu (approvingly) as follows: "Were the power of judging joined with the legislative, the life and liberty of the subject would be exposed to arbitrary controul, for *the judge* would then be *the legislator*."[6] I do not suggest that Madison was saying that common-law lawmaking violated the separation of powers. He wrote in an era when the prevailing image of the common law was that of a preexisting body of rules, uniform throughout the nation (rather than different from state to state), that judges merely "discovered" rather than created. It is only in this century, with the rise of legal realism, that we came to acknowledge that judges in fact "make" the common law, and that each state has its own.

I do suggest, however, that once we have taken this realistic view of what common-law courts do, the uncomfortable relationship of common-law lawmaking to democracy (if not to the technical doctrine of the separation of powers) becomes apparent. Indeed, that was evident to many even before legal realism carried the day. It was one of the principal motivations behind the law-codification movement of the nineteenth century, associated most prominently with the name of David Dudley Field, but espoused by many other avid reformers as well. Consider what one of them, Robert Rantoul, had to say in a Fourth-of-July address in Scituate, Massachusetts, in 1836:

> Judge-made law is ex post facto law, and therefore unjust. An act is not forbidden by the statute law, but it becomes void by judicial construction. The legislature could not effect this, for the Constitution forbids it. The judiciary shall not usurp legislative power, says the Bill of Rights: yet it not only usurps, but runs riot beyond the confines of legislative power.

[6] *The Federalist* No. 47, at 326 (James Madison) (Jacob E. Cooke ed., 1961) (emphasis in original). The reference is to Montesquieu, 1 *The Spirit of the Laws* 152 (Thomas Nugent trans., Hafner Pub. Co., N.Y. 1949).

Judge-made law is special legislation. The judge is human, and feels the bias which the coloring of the particular case gives. If he wishes to decide the next case differently, he has only to distinguish, and thereby make a new law. The legislature must act on general views, and prescribe at once for a whole class of cases.[7]

This is just by way of getting warmed up. Rantoul continues, after observing that the common law "has been called the perfection of human reason":

The Common Law is the perfection of human reason,—just as alcohol is the perfection of sugar. The subtle spirit of the Common Law is reason double distilled, till what was wholesome and nutritive becomes rank poison. Reason is sweet and pleasant to the unsophisticated intellect; but this sublimated perversion of reason bewilders, and perplexes, and plunges its victims into mazes of error.

The judge makes law, by extorting from precedents something which they do not contain. He extends his precedents, which were themselves the extension of others, till, by this accommodating principle, a whole system of law is built up without the authority or interference of the legislator.[8]

The nineteenth-century codification movement espoused by Rantoul and Field was generally opposed by the bar, and hence did not achieve substantial success, except in one field: civil procedure, the law governing the trial of civil cases.[9] (I have always found it curious, by the way, that the only field in which lawyers and judges were willing to abandon judicial lawmaking

---

[7] Robert Rantoul, Oration at Scituate (July 4, 1836), *in* Kermit L. Hall et al., *American Legal History* 317, 317–18 (1991).

[8] *Id.* at 318.

[9] The country's first major code of civil procedure, known as the Field Code (after David Dudley Field, who played a major role in its enactment), was passed in New York in 1848. By the end of the nineteenth century, similar codes had been adopted in many states. *See* Lawrence M. Friedman, *A History of American Law* 340–47 (1973).

11

was a field important to nobody except litigants, lawyers, and judges. Civil procedure used to be the *only* statutory course taught in first-year law school.) Today, generally speaking, the old private-law fields—contracts, torts, property, trusts and estates, family law—remain firmly within the control of state common-law courts.[10] Indeed, it is probably true that in these fields judicial lawmaking can be more freewheeling than ever, since the doctrine of *stare decisis* has appreciably eroded. Prior decisions that even the cleverest mind cannot distinguish can nowadays simply be overruled.

My point in all of this is not that the common law should be scraped away as a barnacle on the hull of democracy. I am content to leave the common law, and the process of developing the common law, where it is. It has proven to be a good method of developing the law in many fields—and perhaps the very best method. An argument can be made that development of the bulk of private law by judges (a natural aristocracy, as Madison accurately portrayed them)[11] is a desirable limitation upon popular democracy. Or as the point was more delicately put in the late nineteenth century by James C. Carter of New York, one of the ardent opponents of Field's codification projects, "the question is, shall this growth, development and improvement of the law remain under the guidance of men selected by the people on account of their special qualifications for the work" (i.e., judges) or "be transferred to a numerous legislative body, dis-

---

[10] The principal exception to this statement consists of so-called Uniform Laws, statutes enacted in virtually identical form by all or a large majority of state legislatures, in an effort to achieve nationwide uniformity with respect to certain aspects of some common-law fields. *See, e.g.*, Uniform Commercial Code, 1 U.L.A. 5 (1989); Uniform Marriage and Divorce Act 9A U.L.A. 156 (1987); Uniform Consumer Credit Code, 7A U.L.A. 17 (1985).

[11] "The [members of the judiciary department], by the mode of their appointment, as well as by the nature and permanency of it, are too far removed from the people to share much in their prepossessions." *The Federalist* No. 49, at 341 (Jacob E. Cooke ed., 1961).

qualified by the nature of their duties for the discharge of this supreme function?"[12]

But though I have no quarrel with the common law and its process, I do question whether the *attitude* of the common-law judge—the mind-set that asks, "What is the most desirable resolution of this case, and how can any impediments to the achievement of that result be evaded?"—is appropriate for most of the work that I do, and much of the work that state judges do. We live in an age of legislation, and most new law is statutory law. As one legal historian has put it, in modern times "the main business of government, and therefore of law, [is] legislative and executive. . . . Even private law, so-called, [has been] turning statutory. The lion's share of the norms and rules that actually govern[] the country [come] out of Congress and the legislatures. . . . The rules of the countless administrative agencies [are] themselves an important, even crucial, source of law."[13] This is particularly true in the federal courts, where, with a qualification so small it does not bear mentioning, there is no such thing as common law. Every issue of law resolved by a federal judge involves interpretation of text—the text of a regulation, or of a statute, or of the Constitution. Let me put the Constitution to one side for the time being, since many believe that that document is in effect a charter for judges to develop an evolving common law of freedom of speech, of privacy rights, and the like. I think that is wrong—indeed, as I shall discuss below, I think it frustrates the whole purpose of a written constitution. But we need not pause to debate that point now, since a very small proportion of judges' work is constitutional interpretation in any event. (Even in the Supreme Court, I would estimate that well less than a fifth of the issues we confront are constitutional issues—and probably less than a twentieth if you exclude criminal-law cases.) By far the greatest part of what I

[12] James C. Carter, *The Proposed Codification of Our Common Law* 87 (New York: Evening Post Printing Office 1884).

[13] Friedman, *supra* note 9, at 590.

13

and all federal judges do is to interpret the meaning of federal statutes and federal agency regulations. Thus the subject of statutory interpretation deserves study and attention in its own right, as the principal business of judges and (hence) lawyers. It will not do to treat the enterprise as simply an inconvenient modern add-on to the judge's primary role of common-law lawmaker. Indeed, attacking the enterprise with the Mr. Fix-it mentality of the common-law judge is a sure recipe for incompetence and usurpation.

THE SCIENCE OF STATUTORY INTERPRETATION

The state of the science of statutory interpretation in American law is accurately described by a prominent treatise on the legal process as follows:

> Do not expect anybody's theory of statutory interpretation, whether it is your own or somebody else's, to be an accurate statement of what courts actually do with statutes. The hard truth of the matter is that American courts have no intelligible, generally accepted, and consistently applied theory of statutory interpretation.[14]

Surely this is a sad commentary: We American judges have no intelligible theory of what we do most.

Even sadder, however, is the fact that the American bar and American legal education, by and large, are unconcerned with the fact that we have no intelligible theory. Whereas legal scholarship has been at pains to rationalize the common law—to devise the *best* rules governing contracts, torts, and so forth—it has been seemingly agnostic as to whether there is even any such thing as good or bad rules of statutory interpretation. There are few law-school courses on the subject, and certainly no required

[14] Henry M. Hart, Jr. & Albert M. Sacks, *The Legal Process* 1169 (William N. Eskridge, Jr. & Philip P. Frickey eds., 1994).

ones; the science of interpretation (if it is a science) is left to be picked up piecemeal, through the reading of cases (good and bad) in substantive fields of law that happen to involve statutes, such as securities law, natural resources law, and employment law.

There is to my knowledge only one treatise on statutory interpretation that purports to treat the subject in a systematic and comprehensive fashion—compared with about six or so on the substantive field of contracts alone. That treatise is Sutherland's *Statutes and Statutory Construction*, first published in 1891, and updated by various editors since, now embracing some eight volumes. As its size alone indicates, it is one of those law books that functions primarily not as a teacher or adviser, but as a litigator's research tool and expert witness—to say, and to lead you to cases that say, why the statute should be interpreted the way your client wants. Despite the fact that statutory interpretation has increased enormously in importance, it is one of the few fields where we have a drought rather than a glut of treatises—fewer than we had fifty years ago, and many fewer than a century ago. The last such treatise, other than Sutherland, was Professor Crawford's one-volume work, *The Construction of Statutes*, published more than half a century ago (1940). Compare that with what was available in the last quarter or so of the nineteenth century, which had, in addition to Sutherland's original 1891 treatise, a *Handbook on the Construction and Interpretation of the Laws* by Henry Campbell Black (author of *Black's Law Dictionary*), published in 1896; *A Commentary on the Interpretation of Statutes* by G. A. Endlich, published in 1888, an Americanized version of Sir Peter Maxwell's 1875 English treatise on the subject; the 1882 *Commentaries on the Written Laws and Their Interpretation* by Joel Prentiss Bishop; the 1874 second edition of Sedgwick's *A Treatise on the Rules Which Govern the Interpretation and Construction of Statutory and Constitutional Law*; and the 1871 Potter's *Dwarris on Statutes*, an Americanized edition by Platt Potter of Sir Fortunatus Dwarris's influential English work.

"INTENT OF THE LEGISLATURE"

Statutory interpretation is such a broad subject that the substance of it cannot be discussed comprehensively here. It is worth examining a few aspects, however, if only to demonstrate the great degree of confusion that prevails. We can begin at the most fundamental possible level. So utterly unformed is the American law of statutory interpretation that not only is its methodology unclear, but even its very *objective* is. Consider the basic question: What are we looking for when we construe a statute?

You will find it frequently said in judicial opinions of my court and others that the judge's objective in interpreting a statute is to give effect to "the intent of the legislature." This principle, in one form or another, goes back at least as far as Blackstone.[15] Unfortunately, it does not square with some of the (few) generally accepted concrete rules of statutory construction. One is the rule that when the text of a statute is clear, that is the end of the matter. Why should that be so, if what the legislature *intended*, rather than what it *said*, is the object of our inquiry? In selecting the words of the statute, the legislature might have misspoken. Why not permit that to be demonstrated from the floor debates? Or indeed, why not accept, as proper material for the court to consider, later explanations by the legislators—a sworn affidavit signed by the majority of each house, for example, as to what they *really* meant?

Another accepted rule of construction is that ambiguities in a newly enacted statute are to be resolved in such fashion as to make the statute, not only internally consistent, but also compatible with previously enacted laws. We simply assume, for purposes of our search for "intent," that the enacting legislature was aware of all those other laws. Well of course that is a fiction,

[15] *See* 1 William Blackstone, *Commentaries on the Laws of England* 59–62, 91 (photo. reprint 1979) (1765).

and if we were really looking for the subjective intent of the enacting legislature we would more likely find it by paying attention to the text (and legislative history) of the new statute in isolation.

The evidence suggests that, despite frequent statements to the contrary, we do not really look for subjective legislative intent. We look for a sort of "objectified" intent—the intent that a reasonable person would gather from the text of the law, placed alongside the remainder of the *corpus juris*. As Bishop's old treatise nicely put it, elaborating upon the usual formulation: "[T]he primary object of all rules for interpreting statutes is to ascertain the legislative intent; *or, exactly, the meaning which the subject is authorized to understand the legislature intended*."[16] And the reason we adopt this objectified version is, I think, that it is simply incompatible with democratic government, or indeed, even with fair government, to have the meaning of a law determined by what the lawgiver meant, rather than by what the lawgiver promulgated. That seems to me one step worse than the trick the emperor Nero was said to engage in: posting edicts high up on the pillars, so that they could not easily be read. Government by unexpressed intent is similarly tyrannical. It is the *law* that governs, not the intent of the lawgiver. That seems to me the essence of the famous American ideal set forth in the Massachusetts constitution: A government of laws, not of men. Men may intend what they will; but it is only the laws that they enact which bind us.

In reality, however, if one accepts the principle that the object of judicial interpretation is to determine the intent of the legislature, being bound by genuine but unexpressed legislative intent rather than the law is only the *theoretical* threat. The *practical* threat is that, under the guise or even the self-delusion of pursuing unexpressed legislative intents, common-law judges will in

---

[16] Joel Prentiss Bishop, *Commentaries on the Written Laws and Their Interpretation* 57–58 (Boston: Little, Brown, & Co. 1882) (emphasis added) (citation omitted).

fact pursue their own objectives and desires, extending their lawmaking proclivities from the common law to the statutory field. When you are told to decide, not on the basis of what the legislature said, but on the basis of what it *meant*, and are assured that there is no necessary connection between the two, your best shot at figuring out what the legislature meant is to ask yourself what a wise and intelligent person *should* have meant; and that will surely bring you to the conclusion that the law means what you think it *ought* to mean—which is precisely how judges decide things under the common law. As Dean Landis of Harvard Law School (a believer in the search for legislative intent) put it in a 1930 article:

> [T]he gravest sins are perpetrated in the name of the intent of the legislature. Judges are rarely willing to admit their role as actual lawgivers, and such admissions as are wrung from their unwilling lips lie in the field of common and not statute law. To condone in these instances the practice of talking in terms of the intent of the legislature, as if the legislature had attributed a particular meaning to certain words, when it is apparent that the intent is that of the judge, is to condone atavistic practices too reminiscent of the medicine man.[17]

CHURCH OF THE HOLY TRINITY

To give some concrete form to the danger I warn against, let me describe what I consider to be the prototypical case involving the triumph of supposed "legislative intent" (a handy cover for judicial intent) over the text of the law. It is called *Church of the Holy Trinity* v. *United States*[18] and was decided by the Supreme Court of the United States in 1892. The Church of the Holy Trinity, located in New York City, contracted with an Englishman to

---

[17] James M. Landis, *A Note on "Statutory Interpretation,"* 43 Harv. L. Rev. 886, 891 (1930).

[18] 143 U.S. 457 (1892).

come over to be its rector and pastor. The United States claimed that this agreement violated a federal statute that made it unlawful for any person to "in any way assist or encourage the importation or migration of any alien . . . into the United States, . . . under contract or agreement . . . made previous to the importation or migration of such alien . . . , to perform labor or service of any kind in the United States . . . ." The Circuit Court for the Southern District of New York held the church liable for the fine that the statute provided. The Supreme Court reversed. The central portion of its reasoning was as follows:

> It must be conceded that the act of the [church] is within the letter of this section, for the relation of rector to his church is one of service, and implies labor on the one side with compensation on the other. Not only are the general words labor and service both used [in the statute], but also, as it were to guard against any narrow interpretation and emphasize a breadth of meaning, to them is added "of any kind;" and, further, . . . the fifth section [of the statute], which makes specific exceptions, among them professional actors, artists, lecturers, singers and domestic servants, strengthens the idea that every other kind of labor and service was intended to be reached by the first section. While there is great force to this reasoning, we cannot think Congress intended to denounce with penalties a transaction like that in the present case. It is a familiar rule, that a thing may be within the letter of the statute and yet not within the statute, because not within its spirit, nor within the intention of its makers.[19]

The Court proceeds to conclude from various extratextual indications, including even a snippet of legislative history (highly unusual in those days), that the statute was intended to apply only to *manual* labor—which renders the exceptions for actors, artists, lecturers, and singers utterly inexplicable. The Court then shifts gears and devotes the last seven pages of its opinion to a lengthy description of how and why we are a religious

---

[19] *Id.* at 458–59.

nation. That being so, it says, "[t]he construction invoked cannot be accepted as correct."[20] It concludes:

> It is a case where there was presented a definite evil, in view of which the legislature used general terms with the purpose of reaching all phases of that evil, and thereafter, unexpectedly, it is developed that the general language thus employed is broad enough to reach cases and acts which the whole history and life of the country affirm could not have been intentionally legislated against. It is the duty of the courts, under those circumstances, to say that, however broad the language of the statute may be, the act, although within the letter, is not within the intention of the legislature, and therefore cannot be within the statute.[21]

Well of course I think that the act was within the letter of the statute, and was therefore within the statute: end of case.[22] Congress can enact foolish statutes as well as wise ones, and it is not for the courts to decide which is which and rewrite the former. I acknowledge an interpretative doctrine of what the old writers call *lapsus linguae* (slip of the tongue), and what our modern cases call "scrivener's error," where on the very face of the statute it is clear to the reader that a mistake of expression (rather than of legislative wisdom) has been made. For example, a statute may say "defendant" when only "criminal defendant" (i.e., not "civil defendant") makes sense.[23] The objective import of such a statute is clear enough, and I think it not contrary to sound principles of interpretation, in such extreme cases, to give

---

[20] *Id.* at 472. [21] *Id.*

[22] End of case, that is, insofar as our subject of statutory construction is concerned. As Professor Tribe's comments suggest, see *post*, at 92, it is possible (though I think far from certain) that in its application to ministers the statute was unconstitutional. But holding a provision unconstitutional is quite different from holding that it says what it does not; constitutional doubt may validly be used to affect the interpretation of an ambiguous statute, *see* United States v. Delaware & Hudson Co., 213 U.S. 366, 407–08 (1909), but not to rewrite a clear one, *see* Moore Ice Cream Co. v. Rose, 289 U.S. 373, 379 (1933).

[23] *See* Green v. Bock Laundry Mach. Co., 490 U.S. 504 (1989).

the totality of context precedence over a single word.[24] But to say that the legislature obviously misspoke is worlds away from saying that the legislature obviously overlegislated. *Church of the Holy Trinity* is cited to us whenever counsel wants us to ignore the narrow, deadening text of the statute, and pay attention to the life-giving legislative intent. It is nothing but an invitation to judicial lawmaking.

There are more sophisticated routes to judicial lawmaking than reliance upon unexpressed legislative intent, but they will not often be found in judicial opinions because they are too obvious a usurpation. Calling the court's desires "unexpressed legislative intent" makes everything seem all right. You will never, I promise, see in a judicial opinion the rationale for judicial lawmaking described in Guido Calabresi's book, *A Common Law for the Age of Statutes*. It says:

> [B]ecause a statute is hard to revise once it is passed, laws are governing us that would not and could not be enacted today, and . . . *some* of these laws not only could not be reenacted but also do not fit, are in some sense inconsistent with, our whole legal landscape. . . .
>
> . . . . There is an alternate way of dealing with [this] problem of legal obsolescence: granting to courts the authority to determine whether a statute is obsolete, whether in one way or another it should be consciously reviewed. At times this doctrine would approach granting to courts the authority to treat statutes as if they were no more and no less than part of the common law.[25]

Indeed. Judge Calabresi says that the courts have already, "in a common law way, . . . come to the point of exercising [the law-revising authority he favors] through fictions, subterfuges, and indirection,"[26] and he is uncertain whether they should continue

---

[24] *Id.* at 527 (Scalia, J., concurring).

[25] Guido Calabresi, *A Common Law for the Age of Statutes* 2 (1982) (emphasis in original).

[26] *Id.* at 117.

down that road or change course to a more forthright acknowledgment of what they are doing.

Another modern and forthright approach to according courts the power to revise statutes is set forth in Professor Eskridge's recent book, *Dynamic Statutory Interpretation*. The essence of it is acceptance of the proposition that it is proper for the judge who applies a statute to consider "'not only what the statute means abstractly, or even on the basis of legislative history, but also what it ought to mean in terms of the needs and goals of our present day society.'"[27] The law means what it ought to mean.

I agree with Judge Calabresi (and Professor Eskridge makes the same point) that many decisions can be cited which, by subterfuge, accomplish precisely what Calabresi and Eskridge and other honest nontextualists propose. As I have said, "legislative intent" divorced from text is one of those subterfuges; and as I have described, *Church of the Holy Trinity* is one of those cases. What I think is needed, however, is not rationalization of this process but abandonment of it. It is simply not compatible with democratic theory that laws mean whatever they ought to mean, and that unelected judges decide what that is.

It may well be that the statutory interpretation adopted by the Court in *Church of the Holy Trinity* produced a desirable result; and it may even be (though I doubt it) that it produced the unexpressed result actually intended by Congress, rather than merely the one desired by the Court. Regardless, the decision was wrong because it failed to follow the text. The text is the law, and it is the text that must be observed. I agree with Justice Holmes's remark, quoted approvingly by Justice Frankfurter in his article on the construction of statutes: "Only a day or two ago—when counsel talked of the intention of a legislature, I was indiscreet enough to say I don't care what their intention was. I

[27] William N. Eskridge, Jr., *Dynamic Statutory Interpretation* 50 (1994) (quoting Arthur Phelps, *Factors Influencing Judges in Interpreting Statutes*, 3 Vand. L. Rev. 456, 469 (1950)).

only want to know what the words mean."[28] And I agree with Holmes's other remark, quoted approvingly by Justice Jackson: "We do not inquire what the legislature meant; we ask only what the statute means."[29]

TEXTUALISM

The philosophy of interpretation I have described above is known as textualism. In some sophisticated circles, it is considered simpleminded—"wooden," "unimaginative," "pedestrian." It is none of that. To be a textualist in good standing, one need not be too dull to perceive the broader social purposes that a statute is designed, or could be designed, to serve; or too hidebound to realize that new times require new laws. One need only hold the belief that judges have no authority to pursue those broader purposes or write those new laws.

Textualism should not be confused with so-called strict constructionism, a degraded form of textualism that brings the whole philosophy into disrepute. I am not a strict constructionist, and no one ought to be—though better that, I suppose, than a nontextualist. A text should not be construed strictly, and it should not be construed leniently; it should be construed reasonably, to contain all that it fairly means. The difference between textualism and strict constructionism can be seen in a case my Court decided four terms ago.[30] The statute at issue provided for an increased jail term if, "during and in relation to . . . [a] drug trafficking crime," the defendant "uses . . . a firearm." The defendant in this case had sought to purchase a quantity of cocaine; and what he had offered to give in exchange for

[28] Felix Frankfurter, *Some Reflections on the Reading of Statutes*, 47 Colum. L. Rev. 527, 538 (1947).

[29] Oliver Wendell Holmes, *Collected Legal Papers* 207 (1920), *quoted in* Schwegmann Bros. v. Calvert Distillers Corp., 341 U.S. 384, 397 (1951) (Jackson, J., concurring).

[30] Smith v. United States, 508 U.S. 223 (1993).

the cocaine was an unloaded firearm, which he showed to the drug-seller. The Court held, I regret to say, that the defendant was subject to the increased penalty, because he had "used a firearm during and in relation to a drug trafficking crime." The vote was not even close (6–3). I dissented. Now I cannot say whether my colleagues in the majority voted the way they did because they are strict-construction textualists, or because they are not textualists at all. But a proper textualist, which is to say my kind of textualist, would surely have voted to acquit. The phrase "uses a gun" fairly connoted use of a gun for what guns are normally used for, that is, as a weapon. As I put the point in my dissent, when you ask someone, "Do you use a cane?" you are not inquiring whether he has hung his grandfather's antique cane as a decoration in the hallway.

But while the good textualist is not a literalist, neither is he a nihilist. Words do have a limited range of meaning, and no interpretation that goes beyond that range is permissible. My favorite example of a departure from text—and certainly the departure that has enabled judges to do more freewheeling law-making than any other—pertains to the Due Process Clause found in the Fifth and Fourteenth Amendments of the United States Constitution, which says that no person shall "be deprived of life, liberty, or property without due process of law." It has been interpreted to prevent the government from taking away certain liberties *beyond* those, such as freedom of speech and of religion, that are specifically named in the Constitution. (The first Supreme Court case to use the Due Process Clause in this fashion was, by the way, *Dred Scott*[31]—not a desirable parentage.) Well, it may or may not be a good thing to guarantee additional liberties, but the Due Process Clause quite obviously does not bear that interpretation. By its inescapable terms, it guarantees only process. Property can be taken by the state; liberty can be taken; even life can be taken; but not without the *process* that our traditions require—notably, a validly enacted

---

[31] Dred Scott v. Sandford, 60 U.S. (19 How.) 393, 450 (1857).

law and a fair trial. To say otherwise is to abandon textualism, and to render democratically adopted texts mere springboards for judicial lawmaking.

Of all the criticisms leveled against textualism, the most mindless is that it is "formalistic." The answer to that is, *of course it's formalistic!* The rule of law is *about* form. If, for example, a citizen performs an act—let us say the sale of certain technology to a foreign country—which is prohibited by a widely publicized bill proposed by the administration and passed by both houses of Congress, *but not yet signed by the President*, that sale is lawful. It is of no consequence that everyone knows both houses of Congress and the President wish to prevent that sale. Before the wish becomes a binding law, it must be embodied in a bill that passes both houses and is signed by the President. Is that not formalism? A murderer has been caught with blood on his hands, bending over the body of his victim; a neighbor with a video camera has filmed the crime; and the murderer has confessed in writing and on videotape. We nonetheless insist that before the state can punish this miscreant, it must conduct a full-dress criminal trial that results in a verdict of guilty. Is that not formalism? Long live formalism. It is what makes a government a government of laws and not of men.

CANONS AND PRESUMPTIONS

Textualism is often associated with rules of interpretation called the canons of construction—which have been widely criticized, indeed even mocked, by modern legal commentators. Many of the canons were originally in Latin, and I suppose that alone is enough to render them contemptible. One, for example, is *expressio unius est exclusio alterius*. Expression of the one is exclusion of the other. What it means is this: If you see a sign that says children under twelve may enter free, you should have no need to ask whether your thirteen-year-old must pay. The inclusion of the one class is an implicit exclusion of the other. Another frequently used canon is *noscitur a sociis*, which means, literally, "it is known by its companions." It stands for the principle that a word is given meaning by those around it. If you tell me, "I took the boat out on the bay," I understand "bay" to mean one thing; if you tell me, "I put the saddle on the bay," I understand it to mean something else. Another canon—perhaps representing only a more specific application of the last one—is *ejusdem generis*, which means "of the same sort." It stands for the proposition that when a text lists a series of items, a general term included in the list should be understood to be limited to items of the same sort. For instance, if someone speaks of using "tacks, staples, screws, nails, rivets, and other things," the general term "other things" surely refers to other fasteners.

All of this is so commonsensical that, were the canons not couched in Latin, you would find it hard to believe anyone could criticize them. But in fact, the canons have been attacked as a sham. As Karl Llewellyn put it in a much-cited derisive piece in the 1950 *Vanderbilt Law Review*: "[T]here are two opposing canons on almost every point. An arranged selection is appended. Every lawyer must be familiar with them all: they are still needed tools of argument."[32] Llewellyn appends a list of canons in two columns, the left-hand column headed "Thrust," and the right-hand column "Parry." But if one examines the list, it becomes apparent that there really are not two opposite canons on "almost every point"—unless one enshrines as a canon whatever vapid statement has ever been made by a willful, law-bending judge. For example, the first canon Llewellyn lists under "Thrust," supported by a citation of Sutherland, is "A statute cannot go beyond its text." Hooray for that. He shows as a "Parry," with no citation of either Sutherland or Black (his principal authorities throughout), the following: "To effect its purpose a statute may be implemented beyond its text." That is *not* a generally accepted canon, though I am sure some willful judges have used it—the judges in *Church of the*

---

[32] Karl N. Llewellyn, *Remarks on the Theory of Appellate Decision and the Rules or Canons about How Statutes Are to Be Construed*, 3 Vand. L. Rev. 395, 401 (1950).

Holy Trinity, for example. And even if it were used more than rarely, why not bring to the canons the same discernment that Llewellyn brought to the study of common-law decisions? Throw out the bad ones and retain the good. There are a number of other faux canons in Llewellyn's list, particularly in the "Parry" column. For example, Parry No. 8: "Courts have the power to inquire into real—as distinct from ostensible—purpose." Never heard of it.

Mostly, however, Llewellyn's "Parries" do not contradict the corresponding canon but rather merely show that it is not absolute. For example, Thrust No. 13: "Words and phrases which have received judicial construction before enactment are to be understood according to that construction." Parry: "Not if the statute clearly requires them to have a different meaning." Well, certainly. Every canon is simply *one indication* of meaning; and if there are more contrary indications (perhaps supported by other canons), it must yield. But that does not render the entire enterprise a fraud—not, at least, unless the judge wishes to make it so.

Another aspect of textual interpretation that merits some discussion is the use of certain presumptions and rules of construction that load the dice for or against a particular result. For example, when courts construe criminal statutes, they apply—or should apply, or say they apply—what is known as the "rule of lenity," which says that any ambiguity in a criminal statute must be resolved in favor of the defendant.[33] There is a rule which says that ambiguities in treaties and statutes dealing with Indian rights are to be resolved in favor of the Indians.[34] And a rule, used to devastating effect in the conservative courts of the 1920s and 1930s, that statutes in derogation of the common law are to be narrowly construed.[35] And another rule, used to equally

---

[33] *See* United States v. Bass, 404 U.S. 336, 347–49 (1971).

[34] *See* Montana v. Blackfeet Tribe of Indians, 471 U.S. 759, 766–68 (1985).

[35] *See* Robert C. Reed & Co. v. Krawill Mach. Corp., 359 U.S. 297, 304–05 (1959).

devastating effect in the liberal courts of more recent years, that "remedial statutes" are to be liberally construed to achieve their "purposes."[36] There is a rule that waivers of sovereign immunity are to be narrowly construed.[37] And a rule that it requires an "unmistakably clear statement" for a federal statute to eliminate state sovereign immunity.[38]

To the honest textualist, all of these preferential rules and presumptions are a lot of trouble. It is hard enough to provide a uniform, objective answer to the question whether a statute, on balance, more reasonably means one thing than another. But it is virtually impossible to expect uniformity and objectivity when there is added, on one or the other side of the balance, a thumb of indeterminate weight. How "narrow" is the narrow construction that certain types of statute are to be accorded; how clear does a broader intent have to be in order to escape it? Every statute that comes into litigation is to some degree "ambiguous"; how ambiguous does ambiguity have to be before the rule of lenity or the rule in favor of Indians applies? How implausible an implausibility can be justified by the "liberal construction" that is supposed to be accorded remedial statutes? And how clear is an "unmistakably clear" statement? There are no answers to these questions, which is why these artificial rules increase the unpredictability, if not the arbitrariness, of judicial decisions. Perhaps for some of the rules that price is worth it. There are worse things than unpredictability and occasional arbitrariness. Perhaps they are a fair price to pay for preservation of the principle that one should not be held criminally liable for an act that is not clearly proscribed; or the principle that federal interference with state sovereign immunity is an extraordinary intrusion.

But whether these dice-loading rules are bad or good, there

---

[36] *See* Tcherepnin v. Knight, 389 U.S. 332, 336 (1967). For more on my aversion to this particular rule, see Antonin Scalia, *Assorted Canards of Contemporary Legal Analysis*, 40 Case W. Res. L. Rev. 581, 581–86 (1990).

[37] *See* United States v. Nordic Village, Inc., 503 U.S. 30, 33–34 (1992).

[38] *See* Dellmuth v. Muth, 491 U.S. 223, 230 (1989).

is also the question of where the courts get the authority to impose them. Can we really just decree that we will interpret the laws that Congress passes to mean less or more than what they fairly say? I doubt it. The rule of lenity is almost as old as the common law itself,[39] so I suppose that is validated by sheer antiquity. The others I am more doubtful about. The rule that statutes in derogation of the common law will be narrowly construed seems like a sheer judicial power-grab. Some of the rules, perhaps, can be considered merely an exaggerated statement of what normal, no-thumb-on-the-scales interpretation would produce anyway. For example, since congressional elimination of state sovereign immunity is such an extraordinary act, one would normally expect it to be explicitly decreed rather than offhandedly implied—so something like a "clear statement" rule is merely normal interpretation. And the same, perhaps, with waiver of sovereign immunity.

LEGISLATIVE HISTORY

Let me turn now from canons and presumptions, which have long been used in statutory construction, to an interpretive device whose widespread use is relatively new: legislative history, by which I mean the statements made in the floor debates, committee reports, and even committee testimony, leading up to the enactment of the legislation. My view that the objective indication of the words, rather than the intent of the legislature, is what constitutes the law leads me, of course, to the conclusion that legislative history should not be used as an authoritative

[39] Sir Peter Maxwell writes that the rule dates back to the time when there were over one hundred capital offenses under English law, including "to cut down a cherry-tree in an orchard, or to be seen for a month in the company of gypsies." Sir Peter Benson Maxwell, *On the Interpretation of Statutes* 239 (London: William Maxwell & Son 1875). *See also* United States v. Wiltberger, 18 U.S. (5 Wheat.) 76, 95 (1820) ("The rule that penal laws are to be construed strictly, is perhaps not much less old than construction itself.").

indication of a statute's meaning. This was the traditional English, and the traditional American, practice. Chief Justice Taney wrote:

> In expounding this law, the judgment of the court cannot, in any degree, be influenced by the construction placed upon it by individual members of Congress in the debate which took place on its passage, nor by the motives or reasons assigned by them for supporting or opposing amendments that were offered. The law as it passed is the will of the majority of both houses, *and the only mode in which that will is spoken is in the act itself*; and we must gather their intention from the language there used, comparing it, when any ambiguity exists, with the laws upon the same subject, and looking, if necessary, to the public history of the times in which it was passed.[40]

That uncompromising view generally prevailed in this country until the present century. The movement to change it gained momentum in the late 1920s and 1930s, driven, believe it or not, by frustration with common-law judges' use of "legislative intent" and phonied-up canons to impose their own views—in those days views opposed to progressive social legislation. I quoted earlier an article by Dean Landis inveighing against such judicial usurpation. The solution he proposed was not the banishment of legislative intent as an interpretive criterion, but rather the use of legislative history to place that intent beyond manipulation.[41]

Extensive use of legislative history in this country dates only from about the 1940s. It was still being criticized by such respected justices as Frankfurter and Jackson as recently as the 1950s. Jackson, for example, wrote in one concurrence:

> I should concur in this result more readily if the Court could reach it by analysis of the statute instead of by psychoanalysis of Congress. When we decide from legislative history, including

[40] Aldridge v. Williams, 44 U.S. (3 How.) 9, 24 (1845) (emphasis added).
[41] *See* Landis, *supra* note 17, at 891–92.

statements of witnesses at hearings, what Congress probably had in mind, we must put ourselves in the place of a majority of Congressmen and act according to the impression we think this history should have made on them. Never having been a Congressman, I am handicapped in that weird endeavor. That process seems to me not interpretation of a statute but creation of a statute.[42]

In the past few decades, however, we have developed a legal culture in which lawyers routinely—and I do mean routinely—make no distinction between words in the text of a statute and words in its legislative history. My Court is frequently told, in briefs and in oral argument, that "Congress said thus-and-so"—when in fact what is being quoted is not the law promulgated by Congress, nor even any text endorsed by a single house of Congress, but rather the statement of a single committee of a single house, set forth in a committee report. Resort to legislative history has become so common that lawyerly wags have popularized a humorous quip inverting the oft-recited (and oft-ignored) rule as to when its use is appropriate: "One should consult the text of the statute," the joke goes, "only when the legislative history is ambiguous." Alas, that is no longer funny. Reality has overtaken parody. A few terms ago, I read a brief that *began* the legal argument with a discussion of legislative history and then continued (I am quoting it verbatim): "Unfortunately, the legislative debates are not helpful. Thus, we turn to the other guidepost in this difficult area, statutory language."[43]

As I have said, I object to the use of legislative history on principle, since I reject intent of the legislature as the proper criterion of the law. What is most exasperating about the use of legislative history, however, is that it does not even make sense for

[42] United States v. Public Utils. Comm'n of Cal., 345 U.S. 295, 319 (1953) (Jackson, J., concurring).

[43] Brief for Petitioner at 21, Jett v. Dallas Indep. Sch. Dist., 491 U.S. 701 (1989), *quoted in* Green v. Bock Laundry Machine Co., 490 U.S. 504, 530 (1989) (Scalia, J., concurring).

those who *accept* legislative intent as the criterion. It is much more likely to produce a false or contrived legislative intent than a genuine one. The first and most obvious reason for this is that, with respect to 99.99 percent of the issues of construction reaching the courts, there *is* no legislative intent, so that any clues provided by the legislative history are bound to be false. Those issues almost invariably involve points of relative detail, compared with the major sweep of the statute in question. That a majority of both houses of Congress (never mind the President, if he signed rather than vetoed the bill) entertained *any* view with regard to such issues is utterly beyond belief. For a virtual certainty, the majority was blissfully unaware of the *existence* of the issue, much less had any preference as to how it should be resolved.

But assuming, contrary to all reality, that the search for "legislative intent" is a search for something that exists, that something is not likely to be found in the archives of legislative history. In earlier days, when Congress had a smaller staff and enacted less legislation, it might have been possible to believe that a significant number of senators or representatives were present for the floor debate, or read the committee reports, and actually voted on the basis of what they heard or read. Those days, if they ever existed, are long gone. The floor is rarely crowded for a debate, the members generally being occupied with committee business and reporting to the floor only when a quorum call is demanded or a vote is to be taken. And as for committee reports, it is not even certain that the members of the issuing *committees* have found time to read them, as demonstrated by the following Senate floor debate on a tax bill, which I had occasion to quote in an opinion written when I was on the Court of Appeals:

> MR. ARMSTRONG. . . . My question, which may take [the chairman of the Committee on Finance] by surprise, is this: Is it the intention of the chairman that the Internal Revenue Service and the Tax Court and other courts take guidance as to the inten-

tion of Congress from the committee report which accompanies this bill?

MR. DOLE. I would certainly hope so . . . .

MR. ARMSTRONG. Mr. President, will the Senator tell me whether or not he wrote the committee report?

MR. DOLE. Did I write the committee report?

MR. ARMSTRONG. Yes.

MR. DOLE. No; the Senator from Kansas did not write the committee report.

MR. ARMSTRONG. Did any Senator write the committee report?

MR. DOLE. I have to check.

MR. ARMSTRONG. Does the Senator know of any Senator who wrote the committee report?

MR. DOLE. I might be able to identify one, but I would have to search. I was here all during the time it was written, I might say, and worked carefully with the staff as they worked. . . .

MR. ARMSTRONG. Mr. President, has the Senator from Kansas, the chairman of the Finance Committee, read the committee report in its entirety?

MR. DOLE. I am working on it. It is not a bestseller, but I am working on it.

MR. ARMSTRONG. Mr. President, did members of the Finance Committee vote on the committee report?

MR. DOLE. No.

MR. ARMSTRONG. Mr. President, the reason I raise the issue is not perhaps apparent on the surface, and let me just state it: . . . . The report itself is not considered by the Committee on Finance. It was not subject to amendment by the Committee on Finance. It is not subject to amendment now by the Senate.

. . . .

. . . If there were matter within this report which was disagreed to by the Senator from Colorado or even by a majority of all Senators, there would be no way for us to change the report. I could not offer an amendment tonight to amend the committee report.

33

> ... [F]or any jurist, administrator, bureaucrat, tax practitioner, or others who might chance upon the written record of this proceeding, let me just make the point that this is not the law, it was not voted on, it is not subject to amendment, and we should discipline ourselves to the task of expressing congressional intent in the statute.[44]

Ironically, but quite understandably, the more courts have relied upon legislative history, the less worthy of reliance it has become. In earlier days, it was at least genuine and not contrived—a real part of the legislation's *history*, in the sense that it was part of the *development* of the bill, part of the attempt to inform and persuade those who voted. Nowadays, however, when it is universally known and expected that judges will resort to floor debates and (especially) committee reports as authoritative expressions of "legislative intent," affecting the courts rather than informing the Congress has become the primary purpose of the exercise. It is less that the courts refer to legislative history because it exists than that legislative history exists because the courts refer to it. One of the routine tasks of the Washington lawyer-lobbyist is to draft language that sympathetic legislators can recite in a prewritten "floor debate"—or, even better, insert into a committee report.

There are several common responses to these criticisms. One is "So what, if most members of Congress do not themselves know what is in the committee report. Most of them do not know the details of the legislation itself, either—but that is valid nonetheless. In fact, they are probably more likely to read and understand the committee report than to read and understand the text." That ignores the central point that genuine knowledge is a precondition for the supposed authoritativeness of a committee report, and not a precondition for the authoritativeness of a statute. The committee report has no claim to our attention

[44] 128 Cong. Rec. 16918–19, 97th Cong., 2d Sess. (July 19, 1982), quoted in Hirschey v. Federal Energy Regulatory Comm'n, 777 F.2d 1, 7 n.1 (D.C. Cir. 1985) (Scalia, J., concurring).

except on the assumption that it was the *basis* for the house's vote and thus represents the house's "intent," which we (presumably) are searching for. A statute, however, has a claim to our attention simply because Article I, section 7 of the Constitution provides that since it has been passed by the prescribed majority (*with or without adequate understanding*), it is a law.

Another response simply challenges head-on the proposition that legislative history must reflect congressional thinking: "Committee reports are *not* authoritative because the full house presumably knows and agrees with them, but rather because the full house *wants* them to be authoritative—that is, leaves to its committees the details of its legislation." It may or may not be true that the houses entertain such a desire; the sentiments of Senator Armstrong quoted earlier suggest that it is not. But if it is true, it is unconstitutional. "All legislative Powers herein granted," the Constitution says, "shall be vested in a Congress of the United States, which shall consist of a Senate and House of Representatives."[45] The legislative power is the power to make laws, not the power to make legislators. It is nondelegable. Congress can no more authorize one committee to "fill in the details" of a particular law in a binding fashion than it can authorize a committee to enact minor laws. Whatever Congress has not *itself* prescribed is left to be resolved by the executive or (ultimately) the judicial branch. That is the very essence of the separation of powers. The only conceivable basis for considering committee reports authoritative, therefore, is that they are a genuine indication of the will of the entire house—which, as I have been at pains to explain, they assuredly are not.

I think that Dean Landis, and those who joined him in the prescription of legislative history as a cure for what he called "willful judges," would be aghast at the results a half century later. On balance, it has facilitated rather than deterred decisions that are based upon the courts' policy preferences, rather than neutral principles of law. Since there are no rules as to how

[45] U.S. Const. art. I, 1.

35

much weight an element of legislative history is entitled to, it can usually be either relied upon or dismissed with equal plausibility. If the willful judge does not like the committee report, he will not follow it; he will call the statute not ambiguous enough, the committee report too ambiguous, or the legislative history (this is a favorite phrase) "as a whole, inconclusive." It is ordinarily very hard to demonstrate that this is false so convincingly as to produce embarrassment. To be sure, there are ambiguities involved, and hence opportunities for judicial willfulness, in other techniques of interpretation as well—the canons of construction, for example, which Dean Landis so thoroughly detested. But the manipulability of legislative history has not *replaced* the manipulabilities of these other techniques; it is has *augmented* them. There are still the canons of construction to play with, *and in addition* legislative history. Legislative history provides, moreover, a uniquely broad playing field. In any major piece of legislation, the legislative history is extensive, and there is something for everybody. As Judge Harold Leventhal used to say, the trick is to look over the heads of the crowd and pick out your friends. The variety and specificity of result that legislative history can achieve is unparalleled.

I think it is time to call an end to a brief and failed experiment, if not for reasons of principle then for reasons of practicality. I have not used legislative history to decide a case for, I believe, the past nine terms. Frankly, that has made very little difference (since legislative history is ordinarily so inconclusive). In the only case I recall in which, had I followed legislative history, I *would* have come out the other way, the rest of my colleagues (who *did* use legislative history) did not come out the other way either.[46] The most immediate and tangible change the abandonment of legislative history would effect is this: Judges, lawyers, and clients will be saved an enormous amount of time and expense. When I was head of the Office of Legal Counsel in the

[46] *See* Wisconsin Public Intervenor v. Mortier, 501 U.S. 597 (1991); *id.*, at 616 (Scalia, J., concurring).

Justice Department, I estimated that 60 percent of the time of the lawyers on my staff was expended finding, and poring over, the incunabula of legislative history. What a waste. We did not use to do it, and we should do it no more.

INTERPRETING CONSTITUTIONAL TEXTS

Without pretending to have exhausted the vast topic of textual interpretation, I wish to address a final subject: the distinctive problem of constitutional interpretation. The problem is distinctive, not because special principles of interpretation apply, but because the usual principles are being applied to an unusual text. Chief Justice Marshall put the point as well as it can be put in *McCulloch* v. *Maryland*:

> A constitution, to contain an accurate detail of all the subdivisions of which its great powers will admit, and of all the means by which they may be carried into execution, would partake of the prolixity of a legal code, and could scarcely be embraced by the human mind. It would probably never be understood by the public. Its nature, therefore, requires, that only its great outlines should be marked, its important objects designated, and the minor ingredients which compose those objects be deduced from the nature of the objects themselves.[47]

In textual interpretation, context is everything, and the context of the Constitution tells us not to expect nit-picking detail, and to give words and phrases an expansive rather than narrow interpretation—though not an interpretation that the language will not bear.

Take, for example, the provision of the First Amendment that forbids abridgment of "the freedom of speech, or of the press." That phrase does not list the full range of communicative

[47] McCulloch v. Maryland, 17 U.S. (4 Wheat.) 316, 407 (1819).

expression. Handwritten letters, for example, are neither speech nor press. Yet surely there is no doubt they cannot be censored. In this constitutional context, speech and press, the two most common forms of communication, stand as a sort of synecdoche for the whole. That is not strict construction, but it is reasonable construction.

It is curious that most of those who insist that the drafter's intent gives meaning to a statute reject the drafter's intent as the criterion for interpretation of the Constitution. I reject it for both. I will consult the writings of some men who happened to be delegates to the Constitutional Convention—Hamilton's and Madison's writings in *The Federalist*, for example. I do so, however, not because they were Framers and therefore their intent is authoritative and must be the law; but rather because their writings, like those of other intelligent and informed people of the time, display how the text of the Constitution was originally understood. Thus I give equal weight to Jay's pieces in *The Federalist*, and to Jefferson's writings, even though neither of them was a Framer. What I look for in the Constitution is precisely what I look for in a statute: the original meaning of the text, not what the original draftsmen intended.

But the Great Divide with regard to constitutional interpretation is not that between Framers' intent and objective meaning, but rather that between *original* meaning (whether derived from Framers' intent or not) and *current* meaning. The ascendant school of constitutional interpretation affirms the existence of what is called The Living Constitution, a body of law that (unlike normal statutes) grows and changes from age to age, in order to meet the needs of a changing society. And it is the judges who determine those needs and "find" that changing law. Seems familiar, doesn't it? Yes, it is the common law returned, but infinitely more powerful than what the old common law ever pretended to be, for now it trumps even the statutes of democratic legislatures. Recall the words I quoted earlier from the Fourth-of-July speech of the avid codifier Robert Rantoul:

"The judge makes law, by extorting from precedents something which they do not contain. He extends his precedents, which were themselves the extension of others, till, by this accommodating principle, a whole system of law is built up without the authority or interference of the legislator."[48] Substitute the word "people" for "legislator," and it is a perfect description of what modern American courts have done with the Constitution.

If you go into a constitutional law class, or study a constitutional law casebook, or read a brief filed in a constitutional law case, you will rarely find the discussion addressed to the text of the constitutional provision that is at issue, or to the question of what was the originally understood or even the originally intended meaning of that text. The starting point of the analysis will be Supreme Court cases, and the new issue will presumptively be decided according to the logic that those cases expressed, with no regard for how far that logic, thus extended, has distanced us from the original text and understanding. Worse still, however, it is known and understood that if that logic fails to produce what in the view of the current Supreme Court is the *desirable* result for the case at hand, then, like good common-law judges, the Court will distinguish its precedents, or narrow them, or if all else fails overrule them, in order that the Constitution might mean what it *ought* to mean. Should there be—to take one of the less controversial examples—a constitutional right to die? If so, there is.[49] Should there be a constitutional right to reclaim a biological child put out for adoption by the other parent? Again, if so, there is.[50] If it is good, it is so. Never mind the text that we are supposedly construing; we will smuggle these new rights in, if all else fails, under the Due Process Clause (which, as I have described, is textually incapable of containing them). Moreover, what the Constitution meant

[48] Rantoul, *supra* note 7, at 318.

[49] *See* Cruzan v. Director, Mo. Dep't of Health, 497 U.S. 261, 279 (1990).

[50] *See In re* Kirchner, 649 N.E.2d 324, 333 (Ill.), *cert. denied*, 115 S. Ct. 2599 (1995).

yesterday it does not necessarily mean today. As our opinions say in the context of our Eighth Amendment jurisprudence (the Cruel and Unusual Punishments Clause), its meaning changes to reflect "the evolving standards of decency that mark the progress of a maturing society."[51]

This is preeminently a common-law way of making law, and not the way of construing a democratically adopted text. I mentioned earlier a famous English treatise on statutory construction called *Dwarris on Statutes*. The fourth of Dwarris's Maxims was as follows: "An act of Parliament cannot alter by reason of time; but the common law may, since *cessante ratione cessat lex*."[52] This remains (however much it may sometimes be evaded) the formally enunciated rule for statutory construction: statutes do not change. Proposals for "dynamic statutory construction," such as those of Judge Calabresi and Professor Eskridge, are concededly avant-garde. The Constitution, however, even though a democratically adopted text, we formally treat like the common law. What, it is fair to ask, is the justification for doing so?

One would suppose that the rule that a text does not change would apply a fortiori to a constitution. If courts felt too much bound by the democratic process to tinker with statutes, when their tinkering could be adjusted by the legislature, how much more should they feel bound not to tinker with a constitution, when their tinkering is virtually irreparable. It certainly cannot be said that a constitution naturally suggests changeability; to the contrary, its whole purpose is to prevent change—to embed certain rights in such a manner that future generations cannot readily take them away. A society that adopts a bill of rights is skeptical that "evolving standards of decency" always "mark progress," and that societies always "mature," as opposed to

[51] Rhodes v. Chapman, 452 U.S. 337, 346 (1981), quoting from Trop v. Dulles, 356 U.S. 86, 101 (1958) (plurality opinion).

[52] Fortunatus Dwarris, *A General Treatise on Statutes, with American Notes and Additions by Platt Potter* 122 (Albany, N.Y. 1871).

rot. Neither the text of such a document nor the intent of its framers (whichever you choose) can possibly lead to the conclusion that its only effect is to take the power of changing rights away from the legislature and give it to the courts.

FLEXIBILITY AND LIBERALITY OF
THE LIVING CONSTITUTION

The argument most frequently made in favor of The Living Constitution is a pragmatic one: Such an evolutionary appoach is necessary in order to provide the "flexibility" that a changing society requires; the Constitution would have snapped if it had not been permitted to bend and grow. This might be a persuasive argument if most of the "growing" that the proponents of this approach have brought upon us in the past, and are determined to bring upon us in the future, were the *elimination* of restrictions upon democratic government. But just the opposite is true. Historically, and particularly in the past thirty-five years, the "evolving" Constitution has imposed a vast array of new constraints—new inflexibilities—upon administrative, judicial, and legislative action. To mention only a few things that formerly could be done or not done, as the society desired, but now cannot be done:

- admitting in a state criminal trial evidence of guilt that was obtained by an unlawful search;[53]
- permitting invocation of God at public-school graduations;[54]
- electing one of the two houses of a state legislature the way the United States Senate is elected, i.e., on a basis that does not give all voters numerically equal representation;[55]
- terminating welfare payments as soon as evidence of fraud is

[53] *See* Mapp v. Ohio, 367 U.S. 643 (1961).
[54] *See* Lee v. Weisman, 505 U.S. 577 (1992).
[55] *See* Reynolds v. Sims, 377 U.S. 533 (1964).

41

received, subject to restoration after hearing if the evidence is satisfactorily refuted;[56]

- imposing property requirements as a condition of voting;[57]
- prohibiting anonymous campaign literature;[58]
- prohibiting pornography.[59]

And the future agenda of constitutional evolutionists is mostly more of the same—the creation of *new* restrictions upon democratic government, rather than the elimination of old ones. *Less* flexibility in government, not *more*. As things now stand, the state and federal governments may either apply capital punishment or abolish it, permit suicide or forbid it—all as the changing times and the changing sentiments of society may demand. But when capital punishment is held to violate the Eighth Amendment, and suicide is held to be protected by the Fourteenth Amendment, all flexibility with regard to those matters will be gone. No, the reality of the matter is that, generally speaking, devotees of The Living Constitution do not seek to facilitate social change but to prevent it.

There are, I must admit, a few exceptions to that—a few instances in which, historically, greater flexibility has been the result of the process. But those exceptions serve only to refute another argument of the proponents of an evolving Constitution, that evolution will always be in the direction of greater personal liberty. (They consider that a great advantage, for reasons that I do not entirely understand. All government represents a balance between individual freedom and social order, and it is not true that every alteration of that balance in the direction of greater individual freedom is necessarily good.) But in any case,

[56] *See* Goldberg v. Kelly, 397 U.S. 254 (1970).

[57] *See* Kramer v. Union Free Sch. Dist., 395 U.S. 621 (1969).

[58] *See* McIntyre v. Ohio Elections Comm'n, 115 S. Ct. 1511 (1995).

[59] Under current doctrine, pornography may be banned only if it is "obscene," *see* Miller v. California, 413 U.S. 15 (1973), a judicially crafted term of art that does not embrace material that excites "normal, healthy sexual desires," Brockett v. Spokane Arcades, Inc., 472 U.S. 491, 498 (1985).

the record of history refutes the proposition that the evolving Constitution will invariably enlarge individual rights. The most obvious refutation is the modern Court's limitation of the constitutional protections afforded to property. The provision prohibiting impairment of the obligation of contracts, for example, has been gutted.[60] I am sure that We the People agree with that development; we value property rights less than the Founders did. So also, we value the right to bear arms less than did the Founders (who thought the right of self-defense to be absolutely fundamental), and there will be few tears shed if and when the Second Amendment is held to guarantee nothing more than the state National Guard. But this just shows that the Founders were right when they feared that some (in their view misguided) future generation might wish to abandon liberties that they considered essential, and so sought to protect those liberties in a Bill of Rights. We may *like* the abridgment of property rights and *like* the elimination of the right to bear arms; but let us not pretend that these are not *reductions* of *rights*.

Or if property rights are too cold to arouse enthusiasm, and the right to bear arms too dangerous, let me give another example: Several terms ago a case came before the Supreme Court involving a prosecution for sexual abuse of a young child. The trial court found that the child would be too frightened to testify in the presence of the (presumed) abuser, and so, pursuant to state law, she was permitted to testify with only the prosecutor and defense counsel present, with the defendant, the judge, and the jury watching over closed-circuit television. A reasonable enough procedure, and it was held to be constitutional by my Court.[61] I dissented, because the Sixth Amendment provides that "[i]n *all* criminal prosecutions the accused shall enjoy the right . . . to be confronted with the witnesses against him" (emphasis added). There is no doubt what confrontation meant—or indeed means today. It means face-to-face, not watching from

---

[60] *See* Home Building & Loan Ass'n v. Blaisdell, 290 U.S. 398 (1934).

[61] *See* Maryland v. Craig, 497 U.S. 836 (1990).

43

another room. And there is no doubt what one of the major purposes of that provision was: to induce *precisely* that pressure upon the witness which the little girl found it difficult to endure. It is difficult to accuse someone to his face, particularly when you are lying. Now no extrinsic factors have changed since that provision was adopted in 1791. Sexual abuse existed then, as it does now; little children were more easily upset than adults, then as now; a means of placing the defendant out of sight of the witness existed then as now (a screen could easily have been erected that would enable the defendant to see the witness, but not the witness the defendant). But the Sixth Amendment nonetheless gave *all* criminal defendants the right to *confront* the witnesses against them, because that was thought to be an important protection. The only significant things that *have* changed, I think, are the society's sensitivity to so-called psychic trauma (which is what we are told the child witness in such a situation suffers) and the society's assessment of where the proper balance ought to be struck between the two extremes of a procedure that assures convicting 100 percent of all child abusers, and a procedure that assures acquitting 100 percent of those falsely accused of child abuse. I have no doubt that the society is, as a whole, happy and pleased with what my Court decided. But we should not pretend that the decision did not *eliminate* a liberty that previously existed.

LACK OF A GUIDING PRINCIPLE FOR EVOLUTION

My pointing out that the American people may be satisfied with a reduction of their liberties should not be taken as a suggestion that the proponents of The Living Constitution *follow* the desires of the American people in determining how the Constitution should evolve. They follow nothing so precise; indeed, as a group they follow nothing at all. Perhaps the most glaring defect of Living Constitutionalism, next to its incompatibility with the whole antievolutionary purpose of a constitution, is that there is no agreement, and no chance of agreement, upon what is to be the guiding principle of the evolution. *Panta rei* is not a sufficiently informative principle of constitutional interpretation. What is it that the judge must consult to determine when, and in what direction, evolution has occurred? Is it the will of the majority, discerned from newspapers, radio talk shows, public opinion polls, and chats at the country club? Is it the philosophy of Hume, or of John Rawls, or of John Stuart Mill, or of Aristotle? As soon as the discussion goes beyond the issue of whether the Constitution is static, the evolutionists divide into as many camps as there are individual views of the good, the true, and the beautiful. I think that is inevitably so, which means that evolutionism is simply not a practicable constitutional philosophy.

I do not suggest, mind you, that originalists always agree upon their answer. There is plenty of room for disagreement as to what original meaning was, and even more as to how that original meaning applies to the situation before the court. But the originalist at least knows what he is looking for: the original meaning of the text. Often—indeed, I dare say usually—that is easy to discern and simple to apply. Sometimes (though not very often) there will be disagreement regarding the original meaning; and sometimes there will be disagreement as to how that original meaning applies to new and unforeseen phenomena. How, for example, does the First Amendment guarantee of "the freedom of speech" apply to new technologies that did not exist when the guarantee was created—to sound trucks, or to government-licensed over-the-air television? In such new fields the Court must follow the trajectory of the First Amendment, so to speak, to determine what it requires—and assuredly that enterprise is not entirely cut-and-dried but requires the exercise of judgment.

But the difficulties and uncertainties of determining original meaning and applying it to modern circumstances are negligible compared with the difficulties and uncertainties of the philosophy which says that the Constitution *changes*; that the very act which it once prohibited it now permits, and which it once permitted it now forbids; and that the key to that change is unknown and unknowable. The originalist, if he does not have all the answers, has many of them. The Confrontation Clause, for example, requires confrontation. For the evolutionist, on the other hand, every question is an open question, every day a new day. No fewer than three of the Justices with whom I have served have maintained that the death penalty is unconstitutional,[62] *even though its use is explicitly contemplated in the Constitution*. The Due Process Clause of the Fifth and Fourteenth Amendments says that no person shall be deprived of life without due process of law; and the Grand Jury Clause of the Fifth Amendment says that no person shall be held to answer for a capital crime without grand jury indictment. No matter. Under The Living Constitution the death penalty may have *become* unconstitutional. And it is up to each Justice to decide for himself (under no standard I can discern) when that occurs.

In the last analysis, however, it probably does not matter what principle, among the innumerable possibilities, the evolutionist proposes to determine in what direction The Living Constitution will grow. Whatever he might propose, at the end of the day an evolving constitution will evolve the way the majority wishes. The people will be willing to leave interpretation of the Constitution to lawyers and law courts so long as the people believe that it is (like the interpretation of a statute) essentially lawyers' work—requiring a close examination of text, history of the text, traditional understanding of the text, judicial precedent, and so forth. But if the people come to believe that the Constitution is *not* a text like other texts; that it means, not what it says or what it was understood to mean, but what it *should* mean, in light of the "evolving standards of decency that mark the progress of a maturing society"—well, then, they will look

---

[62] *See* Gregg v. Georgia, 428 U.S. 153, 227 (1976) (Brennan, J., dissenting); *id.* at 231 (Marshall, J., dissenting); Callins v. Collins, 114 S. Ct. 1127, 1128 (1994) (Blackmun, J., dissenting from denial of certiorari).

for qualifications other than impartiality, judgment, and lawyerly acumen in those whom they select to interpret it. More specifically, they will look for judges who agree with *them* as to what the evolving standards have evolved to; who agree with *them* as to what the Constitution *ought* to be.

It seems to me that that is where we are heading, or perhaps even where we have arrived. Seventy-five years ago, we believed firmly enough in a rock-solid, unchanging Constitution that we felt it necessary to adopt the Nineteenth Amendment to give women the vote. The battle was not fought in the courts, and few thought that it could be, despite the constitutional guarantee of Equal Protection of the Laws; that provision did not, when it was adopted, and hence did not in 1920, guarantee equal access to the ballot but permitted distinctions on the basis not only of age but of property and of sex. Who can doubt that if the issue had been deferred until today, the Constitution would be (formally) unamended, and the courts would be the chosen instrumentality of change? The American people have been converted to belief in The Living Constitution, a "morphing" document that means, from age to age, what it ought to mean. And with that conversion has inevitably come the new phenomenon of selecting and confirming federal judges, at all levels, on the basis of their views regarding a whole series of proposals for constitutional evolution. If the courts are free to write the Constitution anew, they will, by God, write it the way the majority wants; the appointment and confirmation process will see to that. This, of course, is the end of the Bill of Rights, whose meaning will be committed to the very body it was meant to protect against: the majority. By trying to make the Constitution do everything that needs doing from age to age, we shall have caused it to do nothing at all.

Comment

☆

GORDON S. WOOD

This is very distinguished legal company, and I confess to wondering about my qualifications to be a commentator on Justice Scalia's paper. I do not seem to have too many of them. I have never been to law school, so I have not experienced that intellectual rebirth which Justice Scalia says every first-year law school student experiences. I am not a jurist. I am not a legal philosopher. I am not a law professor. I am not even a legal or constitutional historian. I am just a plain eighteenth-century American historian who happens to have written something on the origins of the Constitution. I am not sure that this suffices. Be that as it may, I am pleased to be included among all these learned lawyers.

I have a good deal of sympathy with the complaint that modern judges have tended to run amok, have become makers rather than simply interpreters of the law, and have come to exercise a degree of authority over our lives that is unparalleled among modern Western nations. During the past generation judges have taken to running school systems and prisons. For a decade or more one federal judge even took upon himself to monitor all faculty appointments at my university—for the sake of justice, of course. I do not know of any country in the world where judges wield as much power in shaping the contours of life as they do in the United States.

It would seem that one cannot be a good democrat, with a small *d*, and think that this is a good thing. Justice Scalia realizes that this kind of judicial authority and lawmaking bears what he calls an uncomfortable relationship to democracy. Federal judges are not elected, and yet they do things that presumably only popularly elected representatives ought to be able to do.

The undemocratic nature of judicial authority is not a new problem for Americans, as Justice Scalia concedes. He mentions the nineteenth-century codification movements as early examples of Americans' attempts to limit their judges' ability to make law by judicial opinions. But the problem goes back further than that. From the very beginning of our colonial history we Americans have struggled over the role of the judiciary. Indeed, one of the major complaints of the American colonists against royal authority in the eighteenth century was the extraordinary degree of discretion exercised by royal judges.

At the Revolution in 1776 Americans sought to severely limit this judicial discretion. Although the story is still largely untold, there were efforts in nearly all the states to weed out useless English statutes and legal technicalities and to simplify and codify parts of the common law. The aim, as Jefferson put it, was to end "the eccentric impulses of whimsical, capricious designing man" and to make the judge "a mere machine."[1] Society, it was said, often with ample quotations from the Italian legal reformer Beccaria, needed "but few laws, and these simple, clear, sensible, and easy in their application to the actions of men."[2] Once the legislatures had clarified and written down the laws, then judges would presumably no longer have any justification for following their own inclinations and pleasure in interpreting the law; they would be required, as South Carolinian William Henry Drayton said in 1778, quoting Beccaria, "to follow the letter of the law." Only then could the people be protected from becoming "slaves to the magistrates."[3] Only scientific codifica-

---

[1] Jefferson to Edmund Pendleton, August 26, 1776, in *Papers of Thomas Jefferson*, ed. Julian P. Boyd et al. (Princeton, 1950–), 1:505.

[2] "On the Present States of America," October 10, 1776, in *American Archives. . .*, ed. Peter Force, 5th ser. (Washington, 1837–1846), 2:969.

[3] Drayton, Speech to General Assembly of S.C., January 20, 1778, in *Principles and Acts of the Revolution in America*, ed. Hezekiah Niles (New York, 1876), 359. For a discussion of the confused state of colonial law and the prevalence

tion and strict judicial observance of the text of the law would free the people from judicial tyranny.

This revolutionary and Enlightenment promise of precise legislative enactment and codification was never lost and continued strong well into the nineteenth century, as Justice Scalia points out. Yet as early as the mid-1780s some Americans began to perceive that writing out the laws in black and white was not going to be as easy as they had expected. The states enacted many statutes and printed many laws but not always in the way reformers like Jefferson had wanted. Annually elected, unstable, and logrolling democratic legislatures broke apart plans for comprehensive codes and enacted statutes in such a confused and piecemeal manner that the purpose of simplicity and clarification was defeated; "for every new law ... acts as rubbish, under which we bury the former."[4] Consequently, judicial discretion became more essential and more prevalent in the years following the Revolution than it had been in the colonial period. More statutes were passed than anyone could keep up with; in fact, complained James Madison in 1786, there were more laws enacted in the decade following the Declaration of Independence than had been enacted in the entire previous century of colonial history.

By the 1780s many Americans were already doubting their earlier confidence in their democratically elected legislatures to codify the law and began reevaluating their earlier hostility to judicial power and discretion. When particular statutes had to be enacted for every circumstance, said Connecticut clergyman Moses Mather in 1781, the laws proliferated and resulted in a confusion that wicked men turned to their private advantage. All the legislature really should do was enact a few plain equitable rules and leave their interpretation to the courts. "Indeed,"

---

of judicial discretion see Gordon S. Wood, *The Creation of the American Republic, 1776–1787* (Chapel Hill, 1969), 291–305.

[4] *Rudiments of Law and Government, Deduced from the Law of Nature* (Charleston, S.C., 1783), 35–37.

said Mather, "where civil justice is to be administered not by particular statutes, but by the application of general rules of equity, much will depend upon the wisdom and integrity of the judges."[5] This was a far cry from the Beccarian reformist sentiments of 1776 and showed how far experience had changed American thinking since the Declaration of Independence.

During the 1780s much of the Americans' earlier trust in their democratically elected assemblies, based on generations of colonial experience, was undermined. Many Americans now concluded that their state legislatures not only were incapable of simplifying and codifying the law but, even more alarming, had become the main source of tyranny and injustice in the society. At the same time more and more Americans began looking to the once-feared judiciary as a principal means of restraining these wild and rampaging popular legislatures. William Plumer, a future United States senator and governor of New Hampshire, concluded as early as 1786 that the very "existence" of America's elective governments had come to depend upon the judiciary: "that is the only body of men who will have an effective check upon a numerous Assembly."[6]

In the massive rethinking that took place in the 1780s nearly all parts of America's governments were reformed and reconstituted—reforms and reconstitutions often justified by ingenious manipulations of Montesquieu's doctrine of "separation of powers." But the part of government that benefited most from the rethinking and remodeling of the 1780s was the judiciary. There in the decade following the Revolution was begun the remarkable transformation of the judges from much-feared appendages of crown power into one of "the three capital powers of Government"—from minor magistrates tied to the colonial royal executives into an equal and independent entity in a modern tripartite republican government.[7]

[5] Moses Mather, *Sermon, Preached in the Audience of the General Assembly . . . on the Day of Their Anniversary Election, May 10, 1781* (New London, 1781), 7–8.

[6] Lynn W. Turner, *William Plumer of New Hampshire, 1759–1850* (Chapel Hill, 1962), 34–35.

[7] Address of Mass. Convention (1780), in *The Popular Sources of Political Au-*

The story, amazingly, has never been told. For all our studies of the Supreme Court and its great decisions, we have no history of the emergence of the independent judiciary at the end of the eighteenth and beginning of the nineteenth centuries—perhaps because we take a strong independent judiciary so much for granted. It is a remarkable story, one of the great political and cultural transformations in American history, and it was accompanied by one of the great propaganda efforts in our history. Convincing people that judges appointed for life were an integral and independent part of America's democratic governments—equal in status and authority to the popularly elected executives and legislatures—was an extraordinary accomplishment and one to which many contributed in the decades following the Revolution.

It was not easy. Most eighteenth-century Americans were too fully aware of the modern positivist conception of statutory law, too deeply committed to consent as a basis for law, and from their colonial experience too apprehensive of the possible arbitrariness and uncertainties of judicial discretion to permit themselves easily to give judges independent authority and allow them to interpret and set aside laws made by the elected representatives of the people. "This," said a perplexed James Madison in 1788, "makes the Judiciary Department paramount in fact to the Legislature, which was never intended and can never be proper."[8]

Part of the answer to the dilemma lay in reducing the representative character of the people's agents in the legislatures and enhancing the popularly representative character of the judges. Hamilton attacked this problem directly in *The Federalist* No. 78. The judges, Hamilton argued, had a right to oversee the acts of the presumably sovereign legislatures and to construe statutes and even set some of them aside if they thought they conflicted

---

thority: Documents on the Massachusetts Constitution of 1780, ed. Oscar and Mary Handlin (Cambridge, Mass., 1966), 437.

[8] Madison's Observations on Jefferson's Draft of a Constitution for Virginia, 1788, in Boyd, *Papers of Jefferson*, 6:315.

with either the federal or the state constitution. And the judges could do all this because the legislators were really not the people but only one kind of servant of the people with a limited delegated authority to act on their behalf. Americans, said Hamilton, had no intention of enabling "the representatives of the people to substitute their *will* to that of their constituents." It was in fact "far more rational to suppose, that the courts were designed to be an intermediate body between the people and the legislature, in order, among other things, to keep the latter within the limits assigned to their authority." Hamilton implied, and others drew out the implication much more fully in subsequent years, that the judges, though not elected, resembled the legislators and executives in being agents or servants of the people with a responsibility equal to that of the other two branches of government to carry out the people's will, even to the point of sharing in the making of law. Indeed, just such logic would eventually lead to the election of judges in many states. If the judges were the people's agents, and not the legislators', then by rights they ought to be elected by the people.

Redefining judges as agents of the sovereign people somehow equal in authority with the legislators and executives fundamentally altered the character of the judiciary in America and deeply affected its role in interpreting the law. The courts became independent entities whose relationship with the sovereign people made them appear to have nearly equal authority with the legislatures in the creation of law. The transformation was monumental.[9]

In the colonial period judges had been regarded essentially as appendages or extensions of royal authority embodied in the governors; they were lesser magistrates tied to the governors or chief magistrates. Consequently many colonists concluded that there were really "no more than two powers in any government,

[9] For a recent attempt to draw out the implications of this idea of the courts as agents of the sovereign people, and to apply them to the problem of statutory interpretation, see Carlos E. González, "Reinterpreting Statutory Interpretation," *North Carolina Law Review* 74 (1996): 585–730.

viz. the power to make laws, and the power to execute them; for the judicial power is only a branch of the executive, the chief of every country being the first magistrate."[10] Even John Adams in 1766 regarded "the first grand division of constitutional powers" as "those of legislation and those of execution," with "the administration of justice" resting in "the executive part of the constitution."[11]

As lesser magistracies the colonial courts required special sorts of qualifications for their judges. Men were appointed to the courts not because they had been to law school or had any special legal expertise but because of their social and political rank and influence. And as magistrates they were necessarily involved in politics and governing to an extent that we today find astonishing. Thomas Hutchinson of Massachusetts, for example, who was no lawyer, was in the 1760s chief justice of the superior court, lieutenant governor, a member of the council, and judge of probate of Suffolk County all at the same time. Even after the Constitution was created, some of this older magisterial role of the judges lingered on. During the 1790s both John Jay and Oliver Ellsworth performed diplomatic missions while sitting as justices of the Supreme Court; indeed, while waiting for Jefferson's return from France in 1789, Jay served simultaneously as secretary of state and chief justice of the Supreme Court. Supreme Court justice Samuel Chase saw nothing wrong with his open politicking on behalf of the Federalist cause. Congress in its Invalid Pension Act of 1792 assigned the federal courts administrative and magisterial duties that were not strictly judicial and that were actually subject to review by the secretary of war and the Congress. Of the twenty-eight men who sat on the federal district courts in the 1790s, only eight had held high judicial office in their states; but nearly all of them had been prominent political figures, having served in notable state

[10] *Four Letters on Interesting Subjects* (Philadelphia, 1776), 21.

[11] [Adams], *Boston Gazette*, January 27, 1766, in *Works of John Adams. . .*, ed. Charles F. Adams (Boston, 1850–1856), 3:480–82.

offices and in the Continental Congress. The judges saw their service on the court as simply an extension of their general political activity; some of them even continued to exercise political influence and pass on Federalist patronage in their districts while sitting on the bench. Such judges were political authorities, not professional legal experts.[12]

By the early nineteenth century, however, judges began to shed their traditional broad and ill-defined political and magisterial roles that had previously identified them with the executive branch, and to adopt roles that were much more exclusively legal. The behavior of Chase in politically haranguing juries from the bench or of Jay and Ellsworth in performing diplomatic missions while sitting as justices of the Supreme Court was not duplicated; and in Hayburn's Case of 1792 several justices of the Supreme Court actually protested against the Congress's assigning administrative and magisterial duties to them on the grounds that it violated the separation of powers. Judges withdrew from politics, promoted the development of law as a mysterious science known best by trained experts, and limited their activities to the regular courts, which became increasingly professional and less burdened by popular juries.

This separation of law from politics meant that the courts now tended to avoid the most explosive and partisan political issues. Certainly the Marshall Court succeeded as well as it did because it retreated from the advanced and exposed political positions, including enlarged definitions of treason and of federal jurisdiction over the common law of crimes, that the Federalists had tried to stake out for the national judiciary in the 1790s. As the judges pulled back from politics, however, the courts attempted at the same time to designate other important concerns as particular issues of law that were within their exclusive jurisdiction. Men began to draw lines around what was political or legisla-

[12] Sandra Frances VanBurkleo, "'Honour, Justice, and Interest': John Jay's Republican Politics and Statesmanship on the Federal Bench," *Journal of the Early Republic* 4 (1984): 263–64, 269; Russell Wheeler, "Extrajudicial Activities of the Early Supreme Court," *Supreme Court Review*, 1973, 123–58.

tive and what was legal or judicial, and to justify the distinctions by the doctrine of separation of powers. It is remarkable at times to see the lengths to which some of the Founding Fathers went to justify their new idea of separating adjudication from legislation. As early as 1787 Alexander Hamilton argued in the New York Assembly that the state constitution prevented anyone from being deprived of his rights except "by the law of the land" or, as a recent act of the assembly had put it, "by due process of law," which, said Hamilton in an astonishing and novel twist, had "a precise technical import": these words were now "only applicable to the process and proceedings of the courts of justice; they can never be referred to an act of legislature," even though the legislature had written them.[13] As Marshall said in his Marbury decision, which was crucial in defining this newly reduced but exclusive role for the courts, some questions were political; "they respect the nation, not individual rights," and thus were "only politically examinable." But questions involving the vested rights of individuals were different;

---

[13] Hamilton, Remarks in New York Assembly, February 6, 1787, in *The Papers of Alexander Hamilton*, ed. Harold C. Syrett et al. (New York, 1961–), 4:35. The view expressed by Hamilton did not of course immediately take hold. The attorney general of North Carolina, for example, argued in 1794 that the clauses of the state constitution referring to due process and the law of the land were not limitations on the legislature; they were "declarations the people thought proper to make of their rights, not against a power they supposed their own representatives might usurp, but against oppression and usurpation in general . . . , by a pretended prerogative against or without the authority of law." Thus the assertion that no one could be deprived of his property "except by the law of the land" referred not, as Hamilton would have it, exclusively to judicial proceedings, but simply to "a law for the people of North Carolina, made or adopted by themselves by the intervention of their own legislature." Edward S. Corwin, "The Doctrine of Due Process of Law before the Civil War," *Harvard Law Review* 24 (1911): 371–72. Blackstone had written that one of the absolute rights of individuals was "the right of property: which consists in the free use, enjoyment and disposal of all his acquisitions, without any control or diminution, *save only by the laws of the land*"—which of course for Blackstone included those laws enacted by Parliament. Corwin, "Basic Doctrine of American Constitutional Law," *Michigan Law Review* 12 (1914): 254.

they were in their "nature, judicial, and must be tried by the judicial authority."[14]

Placing legal boundaries around issues such as property rights and contracts had the effect of isolating these issues from popular tampering, partisan debate, and the clashes of interest-group politics. The power to interpret constitutions became a matter not of political interest to be determined by legislatures but of the "fixed principles" of a domesticated constitutional law to be determined by judges alone. Without the protection of the courts and the intricacies of the common law, United States attorney Alexander Dallas of Pennsylvania even argued in 1805, "rights would remain forever without remedies and wrongs without redress." Americans could no longer count on their elected legislatures to solve many of the problems of their lives. "For the varying exigencies of social life, for the complicated interests of an enterprising nation, the positive acts of the legislature can provide little."[15] This seems to be a severe indictment of popular democracy; yet it is so only if we regard legislatures as somehow more representative of the people than the judges. But Hamilton in *The Federalist* No. 78 along with many others had cast doubt on just this point. Judges had acquired an independent standing in American culture which enabled them to do things that no other judges in the world could do.

I relate all this early American history because I think it points up that the problem with which Justice Scalia is dealing is one deeply rooted in our history, and as such it is probably not as susceptible to solution as he implies. Perhaps the enhanced judicial discretion and judicial lawmaking of the past three or four decades represents a change in degree, not one in kind. Justice

[14] *Marbury v. Madison* (1803), in *U.S. Supreme Court Reports*, ed. William Cranch (Washington, 1804), 166, 167.

[15] Alexander J. Dallas, quoted in Richard E. Ellis, *The Jeffersonian Crisis: Courts and Politics in the Young Republic* (New York, 1971), 179; Michael Les Benedict, "Laissez-Faire and Liberty: A Re-Evaluation of the Meaning and Origins of Laissez-Faire Constitutionalism," *Law and History Review* 3 (1985): 323–26.

Scalia may believe that "it is simply not compatible with democratic theory that laws mean whatever they ought to mean, and that unelected judges decide what that is." Yet for good or for ill, judges have exercised that sort of presumably undemocratic authority from the very beginning of our history. We have never had a purely democratic system of government, in any traditional meaning of that term. For this reason, from the very outset a good democratic majoritarian like Jefferson never liked judges and the power they wielded.

Although Justice Scalia apparently is willing to allow the common law to remain as a more or less desirable limitation upon popular democracy, he does want to do something about judicial lawmaking. What really bothers him about the present excess of judicial discretion, or at least what he has chosen to focus on in this paper, is the way in which the common-law attitude or mind-set of judges has been brought into the arena of statutory interpretation. I have no doubt of this issue's importance, but it does seem to me to be only an aspect of the problem that we Americans have with our judges, possibly more a manifestation of the problem than a cause of it. But perhaps because it is an aspect that Justice Scalia can actually do something about on the Court, it is where he wants us to focus our attention.

Let me raise a few questions about this problem of statutory interpretation. First of all, I wonder whether the distinction Justice Scalia has drawn between common-law interpretation and statutory interpretation is not too sharp. In any common-law system statutory construction seems bound to take on many of the characteristics of common-law interpretation. I am not a lawyer, but I do have the sense that English common-law judges, in construing parliamentary statutes try to fit them into the body of the law; in English jurisprudence, then, knowing the text of a statute is not the same as knowing the law. Thus even in England, which has no explicit tradition of judicial review and believes devoutly in the sovereignty of Parliament, judicial interpretation of texts requires extensive knowledge of the whole legal system and involves the continual creation of new legal meanings. This is why English judges have been accused of making the law as a legislator does almost as often as have American judges.

All the legislatures in the English-speaking world began as courts making judgments. The sharp distinction we recognize between legislation and adjudication is a modern one; it essentially emerged in Anglo-American thinking during the seventeenth and eighteenth centuries. Just as the colonial judges thought of themselves as arms of the executive, exercising administrative and magisterial functions, so too did the legislatures often consider themselves to be a kind of court, making judicial-like determinations. In fact, the state legislatures as late as the 1780s were deeply involved in what we would regard as exclusively judicial matters, interfering in causes between private parties, reversing court decisions, and staying executions after judgments.

There was a long history behind this blurring of legislative and judicial matters. Parliament had originally been called the High Court of Parliament, and the Massachusetts legislature was (and is still) called the General Court. Parliamentary statutes or enactments of the General Court of the Massachusetts Bay colony were in effect judgments of the highest court in the land. As such, they were amendments or modifications of the common law; and because they were amendments or modifications of the common law, they had to make sense in terms of the rest of the common law. And it was the responsibility of the lower courts to see that they did. As Chief Justice Coke said in the famous case of Dr. Bonham in 1610, if a statute should turn out to be against the reason of the common law (making a man, for example, a judge in his own cause), then the common law would control it and adjudge such an act to be void. As the highest court, Parliament would have done the same, he said, if it had realized the injustice it had created in this particular instance. In making such a judgment, moreover, Coke was quite willing to try to assess the legislative intent of Parliament in enacting the statute.

Of course, with the emergence in the eighteenth century of the idea of parliamentary sovereignty and the positivist conception of law English judges could no longer claim, as Coke did, the ability to set aside acts of Parliament. But, as W. M. Geldart and his successive editors have pointed out in their authoritative work, *Elements of English Law*, English judges did claim and do claim to have the capacity to interpret and construe parliamentary statutes in such a way as to fit them into the entire legal structure.[16] Thus the English common-law judges, despite having to bow to the sovereignty of Parliament, have been left with an extraordinary amount of room for statutory interpretation and construction. And, as Blackstone pointed out, there were well–worked out rules for judges to follow in construing and interpreting the law—rules that Hamilton in *The Federalist* No. 83 called "rules of *common sense*, adopted by the courts in the construction of the laws." This traditional English interpretative capacity is not American judicial review by any means, but it is something more than judicial passivity. All of this suggests to me that there are very good deeply rooted historical reasons why statutory construction in both England and America has involved a good deal of judicial common-law type interpretation.

I think Justice Scalia is correct in linking the problem of statutory interpretation with constitutional interpretation. For it seems to me that the most important element in the development of judicial review was the treating of the Constitution as a statute—a superstatute no doubt, but nevertheless one that could be interpreted in the ordinary court system. Some of the Founding Fathers, including Jefferson and Madison, tended to conceive of the Constitution as a law that was too fundamental and awesome to be restricted to ordinary judicial interpretation. It was a set of first principles that all departments of the government had a right to interpret; all branches of government had

---

[16] W. M. Geldart, *Elements of English Law*, 6th ed., rev. William Holdsworth and H. G. Hanbury (London, 1959)

what Madison called "a *concurrent* right to expound the constitution."[17] When the several departments disagreed in their understanding of the fundamental law, wrote Madison in *The Federalist* No. 49, "an appeal to the people themselves, . . . can alone declare its true meaning, and enforce its observance."

Other founders, however, culminating in the decisions of the Marshall Court, collapsed the age-old distinction between fundamental and ordinary law—a process that has aptly been called "the legalization of fundamental law."[18] These founders tamed what had hitherto been an object of fearful significance and wonder to the point that it could be routinely interpreted in the ordinary court system. They brought the higher law of the Constitution within the realm of ordinary law and subjected it to the long-standing rules of legal exposition and construction as if it were no different from a lowly statute. In effect, all the wide-ranging power of explication and interpretation traditionally wielded by common-law judges over ordinary statutes in relation to the law could now be applied to the Constitution itself. American judges could now construe the all-too-brief words of the Constitution by the rules of construction that Blackstone had laid down—subject-matter, intention, context, and reasonableness—as if they were the words of an ordinary statute.

Which brings us back to Justice Scalia and statutory interpretation. Justice Scalia is certainly right in stressing the extraordinary degree of discretionary power that American judges now wield and the dangers of that power. But, as I have tried to suggest, that power is the product of immense changes in our legal and judicial culture which have occurred over the past two hundred years, and these changes cannot be easily reversed. His remedy of textualism in interpretation seems scarcely commensurate with the severity of the problem and may in fact be no

[17] Madison, "Helvidius No. II" 1793, in *The Writings of James Madison*, ed. Guillard Hunt (New York, 1900–1910), 6:155.

[18] Sylvia Snowiss, *Judicial Review and the Law of the Constitution* (New Haven, 1990), 64.

solution at all. Textualism, as Justice Scalia defines it, appears to me to be as permissive and as open to arbitrary judicial discretion and expansion as the use of legislative intent or other interpretative methods, if the text-minded judge is so inclined. Ultimately there seems to be no easy way to limit the judges' interpretative power except by changing the attitude of judges themselves (in effect, changing the judicial culture, which is what I suppose Justice Scalia's essay is trying to do), or by appointing to the bench only those judges having the attitude you want.

Perhaps the continual politicizing of judicial appointments will eventually lead to a renewed appreciation of the dangers of mixing law and politics and result in a renewed emphasis on the esoteric and scientifically legal aspects of adjudication. The sharp separation of law from politics made in the early nineteenth century was the secret of Marshall's success, and a similar development may occur in the future. This would not necessarily mean a diminution of the role of judges in our constitutional system, but certainly a new emphasis on technical legalism might work to limit their capacity to take on obvious policy questions and political issues directly. But first I suppose we must reverse some of the reductio ad absurdum tendencies of legal realism and remystify some of what lawyers and judges do. The real source of the judicial problem that troubles Justice Scalia lies in our demystification of the law, which is an aspect of the general demystification of all authority that has taken place in the twentieth century.

For most of us it is still a government of laws, not men. I do not believe that anyone wants the law to be whatever the judge on any particular day happens to feel it ought to be. Even those jurists who want an expanded role for judicial lawmaking are reluctant to promote this role too openly, too explicitly. In that reluctance is the hope for the revival of some semblance of disinterested jurisprudence.

Comment

☆

LAURENCE H. TRIBE

I DO NOT propose to discuss here the entirety of Justice Scalia's remarks about what he perceives to be the lamentable influence of common-law methodology on the enterprise of interpreting statutory and constitutional texts. Rather, I will focus on the enterprise of *constitutional* interpretation in particular, and on my points of agreement with, rejection of, or puzzlement at what Justice Scalia has said in these lectures on that especially significant subject.

Let me begin with my principal area of agreement with Justice Scalia. Like him, I believe that when we ask what a *legal text* means—what it requires of us, what it permits us to do, and what it forbids—we ought *not* to be inquiring (except perhaps very peripherally) into the ideas, intentions, or expectations subjectively held by whatever particular persons were, as a historical matter, involved in drafting, promulgating, or ratifying the text in question. To be sure, those matters, when reliably ascertainable, might shed some light on otherwise ambiguous or perplexing words or phrases—by pointing us, as readers, toward the linguistic frame of reference within which the people to whom those words or phrases were addressed would have "translated" and thus understood them. But such thoughts and beliefs can never substitute for what was in fact *enacted as law*. Like Justice Scalia, I never cease to be amazed by the arguments of judges, lawyers, or others who proceed as though legal texts were little more than interesting documentary evidence of what some lawgiver had in mind. And, like the justice, I find little to

For research assistance, I am grateful to Melanie Oxhorn, J.D. 1994.

commend the proposition that anyone ought, in any circumstances I can imagine, to feel legally bound to obey another's mere wish or thought, or legally bound to act in accord with another's mere hope or fear.

Justice Scalia is by no means always faithful to this approach. Consider, for example, his argument that because the Due Process Clauses of the Fifth and Fourteenth Amendments say that no person shall be deprived of life without due process of law, and the Grand Jury Clause of the Fifth Amendment says that no person shall be held to answer for a capital crime without grand jury indictment, it follows that the death penalty cannot possibly be unconstitutional.[1] Not having come to any final conclusion of my own as to the death penalty's constitutional validity, I would note only that Justice Scalia's conclusion "follows" from the evidence he cites only if one treats as decisive the obvious *expectation* of those writing and ratifying the Constitution from 1787 to 1791, and the Fourteenth Amendment in 1868, that the death penalty would never qualify as a "cruel and unusual punishment" under the Eighth Amendment. But, on Justice Scalia's view, that subjective expectation could not be considered part of the Constitution, because only the text's *meaning*, rather than the unenacted expectations and assumptions of those who wrote or ratified that document, should properly govern constitutional interpretation.

Let us, however, take Justice Scalia at his word and assume that, notwithstanding such counterexamples from his own constitutional jurisprudence, he does indeed believe, as I do, that it is the *text's* meaning, and not the content of anyone's expectations or intentions, that binds us as law. For Justice Scalia, this recognition leads directly to a fork in the road that divides those who follow what he deems the true path of the interpretivist from those who are led astray by the sirens of an evolutionary ideology. Thus Justice Scalia argues that "the Great Divide with regard to constitutional interpretation" of the text is "that be-

---

[1] *See* Scalia, "Common-Law Courts in a Civil-Law System," p. 46.

tween *original* meaning (whether derived from Framers' intent or not) and *current* meaning."[2] He proposes a dichotomy between a mode of textual interpretation that seeks out, neither strictly nor loosely but (by his lights) reasonably, "the original meaning of the text"—"how the text of the Constitution was originally understood"—and a mode (one he describes as currently "ascendant" in the academy and perhaps among lawyers and judges) that looks for (actually, he says, makes up) whatever "meaning" can best "meet the needs of a changing society."[3] The former mode constitutes judging; the latter, lawmaking *disguised* as judging.

It is a familiar dichotomy, and it has been met with a familiar repertoire of replies. Ronald Dworkin, for instance, has responded, both in some of his prior writings[4] and in his reaction to Justice Scalia's lecture, that Justice Scalia has misidentified the *true* Great Divide. We are all originalists now, Dworkin says— all of us (all who matter, anyhow), according to him, are searching for what the text originally meant—but some of us err in seeking that meaning in what the authors or ratifiers intended or expected the *effects* or *consequences* of the text they enacted to be, rather than in what the authors or ratifiers intended to *say* through the text they adopted. For Dworkin, therefore, Justice Scalia's error consists not in fixing his gaze upon the intentions of various people in 1787–1789 (in the case of the original Constitution), or in 1791 (in the case of the Bill of Rights), or in 1868 (in the case of the Fourteenth Amendment), but in looking at the wrong set of intentions—at what those people intended to *do* rather than at what they intended to *say*. Dworkin then proceeds to claim that because they quite *obviously* intended, at least in their more abstract pronouncements (about freedom of speech, due process of law, and the like), to utter broad statements of principle (whose precise application to particular practices

---

[2] *Id.*, p. 38.

[3] *Id. See also id.*, p. 47 (criticizing this view as making the Constitution a "'morphing' document").

[4] *See* Ronald Dworkin, *Law's Empire* (1987).

would have to be worked out by others over time) rather than to utter narrow and dated statements about which government practices are permitted (say, regulating the time, place, or manner of speech in content-neutral and narrowly tailored ways) and which are forbidden (say, licensing the press), it follows that it is he, and not Justice Scalia, who is the *true* originalist.

With part of the Dworkin critique, I certainly agree: Like nearly everyone, I agree, for instance, that the Supreme Court's 1954 decision that official school segregation by race violates equal protection correctly interprets what the Fourteenth Amendment says (and *always* said)—even though it may well defy what the amendment's authors and ratifiers expected the amendment to do[5]—and indeed I agree that the authors and ratifiers themselves may well have intended to enact a provision that might, in light of its broad language and its uncertain reach, end up condemning some of what they then regarded as entirely just and proper. Like Dworkin and many others, I read some of the Constitution's provisions (including, in the case of *Brown* v. *Board of Education*, the provision that states not deprive persons of the "equal protection of the laws") as enacting fairly abstract principles, and others as enacting quite concrete rules.

But I do not agree with either Professor Dworkin or Justice Scalia that one can "discover" which provisions are of which sort either by meditating about the language used or by ascertaining, through accurate use of the tools of history and psychology and biography, the empirical facts about what a finite set of actors at particular moments in our past meant to be saying. Nor do I agree that the level of abstraction or generality at which a constitutional clause or phrase is to be read is normally obvious to the astute reader or user of these tools or, indeed, normally fixed for all time by what a particular group of individuals had

[5] *See* Robert H. Bork, *The Tempting of America* 75–76, 82 (1990) (defending the result in Brown v. Board of Education, notwithstanding his view that those who ratified the Fourteenth Amendment did not think it outlawed segregation).

it in mind to utter. Nor, finally, do I agree that all constitutional provisions may be neatly classified at birth into one or the other of two distinct species, one reserved for broad and dynamic statements of abstract principle that are capable of elaboration and application only through the processes of moral philosophy, and the other reserved for dated, static, and concrete rules whose application does not engage the reader's moral faculties in any significant way.

Perhaps, for example, those who wrote Article I's prohibitions against state and federal "bills of attainder,"[6] or those who ratified these prohibitions, would have said, if asked, that they meant primarily to describe and to prohibit a quite specific sort of enactment—one by which a legislative body would actually name particular individuals and condemn them to exile or death as enemies of the state—rather than to proscribe anything as broad and abstract as "trial by legislature," understood to be any process in which representative bodies inflict stigmatizing deprivations of life, liberty, or property upon closed classes of persons.[7] Yet I agree with the Supreme Court's jurisprudence reading the prohibitions against state and federal bills of attainder to state the latter sort of proscription, and to link it with procedural protections of fair trial as well as with aspects of the separation of powers, rather than merely to forbid the particularly odious ancient practice that the authors and ratifiers might principally have had in mind when they spoke of "bills of attainder."[8] Precisely what the authors and ratifiers of that part of

[6] U.S. Const. art. I, 9, cl. 3; art. I, 10, cl. 1.

[7] *See* John H. Ely, Note, *The Bounds of Legislative Specification: A Suggested Approach to the Bill of Attainder Clause,* 72 Yale L.J. 330 (1962) (urging the broader reading).

[8] *See* Laurence H. Tribe, *American Constitutional Law* 10-1 to 10-6 (2d ed. 1988). Compare Justice Scalia's reading of the words "speech and press" as a 'synecdoche for the whole" of "communication," "Common-Law Courts in a Civil-Law System," p. 38, including modes known in 1791, *id.* ('[h]and-written letters") and modes then unimaginable, *id.,* p. 45 (e.g., "over-the-air television").

69

Article I actually meant to say is, in a sense, lost to us forever and, in another sense, not crucial. For the text they enacted was, through their action, launched upon a historic voyage of interpretation in which succeeding generations, looking at the entire text of the Constitution as amended from time to time, would elaborate what the text means in ways all but certain not to remain static. In any event, regarding the ban on bills of attainder as applicable only to the precise kinds of punitively targeted legislation that people in 1791 consciously contemplated, and construing the Constitution to permit legislative practices that are functionally indistinguishable but do not quite fit the classic model, would create gaps in the Constitution's edifice of protections against legislative trials, and would do so not out of respect for any compromise deliberately reached in the constitution-making process[9] but simply because the document's authors *happened* to describe a form of abuse by reference to a historically tangible subcategory of what they might best be understood to have prohibited. In such circumstances, I would argue that—much as Article I's references to congressional power to raise and support an army and navy should not be read to negate congressional power to launch an air force, and much as the First Amendment's protections of "speech and press" from abridgment by "Congress" should not be read to negate or limit protection from the executive and judicial branches, or protection of film, sculpture, or thought itself—so too Article I's references to bills of attainder, although prohibitory rather than empowering in nature, should not be read to permit laws that share all the basic vices of such bills though not quite all of their historical birthmarks.

So too, perhaps, with other constitutional clauses that some

[9] When such deliberate compromises appear to underlie a constitutional gap or seeming inconsistency—as, for example, with the absence of any ban on *federal* as opposed to *state* laws impairing the obligation of contracts—then fidelity to the entirety of the text and structure of course compels us to construe the document in a manner that honors those compromises rather than seeks to "correct" the perceived "flaws."

have been inclined to read as only codifying narrow rules rather than as also supporting broad principles—including, conceivably, the Second Amendment's seemingly state-milita-based provision dealing with the "right to bear arms,"[10] or the Third Amendment's seemingly limited and specific protection against the "quartering of soldiers,"[11] or the Fourth Amendment's seemingly narrow procedural safeguards against certain kinds of searches and seizures.[12]

The task of deciding which provisions to treat as generative of constitutional principles broader or deeper than their specific terms might at first suggest, and then of deciding just what principles such provisions, read alone or in combination with others, should be taken to enact, lies at the core of the interpretive enterprise. That task cannot properly be discharged as though it were merely an exercise, however grand, in historical reconstruction or simply a foray, however impressive, into mind reading. To prevent that interpretive task from degenerating into the imposition of one's personal preferences or values under the guise of constitutional exegesis, one must concede how difficult the task is; avoid all pretense that it can be reduced to a passive process of *discovering* rather than *constructing* an interpretation; and replace such pretense with a forthright account, incomplete and inconclusive though it might be, of why

[10]*See* Sanford Levinson, *The Embarrassing Second Amendment*, 99 Yale L.J. 637 (1989). Interestingly, Justice Scalia does appear willing to treat the Second Amendment, despite the reference in its preamble to state militias, as embodying some principle about what he refers to as "the right of self-defense." "Common-Law Courts in a Civil-Law System," p. 43.

[11] The right not to have the government put its regiments in one's home might make little sense without some presupposed right not to have the government regiment every detail of what one *does* in one's home. *See* Griswold v. Connecticut, 381 U.S. 479, 484 (1965) (observing that the Third Amendment is "another facet" of privacy).

[12] *See, e.g.*, Akhil Reed Amar, *Fourth Amendment First Principles*, 107 Harv. L. Rev. 757, 785 (1994) (discussing the Fourth Amendment's substantive protection of "the right of the people to be secure in their persons, houses, papers, and effects").

one deems his or her proposed construction of the text to be worthy of acceptance, in light of the Constitution as a whole and the history of its interpretation.

However much undoubtedly *divides* the interpretive approaches of Professor Dworkin and Justice Scalia, what *unites* them is, I fear, a shared failure to adhere to these canons of candor and of self-conscious humility in the face of a task about which none of us is entitled to feel too self-assured. Thus just as I think Justice Scalia errs when he claims to know with confidence that the phrase "freedom of speech"—to take an example that sounds less like a narrow term of art than does "bill of attainder"—was understood at the relevant time, and therefore must be understood today, to refer not to any principle against government censorship but to the rights of Englishmen as of 1791,[13] so too I think Professor Dworkin errs when he claims to know with equal confidence that the phrase was understood then, and therefore must be understood today, to refer instead to a broad moral principle that we may then proceed to elaborate. Both of them err, I think, in the confidence of their conclusions about how various people in fact understood particular phrases a century or two ago; in their certitude about whose understanding counts as decisive;[14] and, above all, in their insistence that they know how that historical fact bears on whether the relevant text expressed a concrete rule or an abstract principle.

In rejecting the no doubt sincere (but nevertheless misguided) certitudes of both of these estimable thinkers, I leave myself exposed, of course, to the charge that I have no genuine "theory"

[13] *See* notes 28–29 and accompanying text, *infra*.

[14] Professor Dworkin's reply to Justice Scalia suggests that he would focus on what various officials understood by the words they wrote or voted to ratify, while Justice Scalia would apparently focus on what a reasonably well-informed citizen of the time would have understood. In his earlier writing, Professor Dworkin elaborated a more nuanced (and, I believe, more defensible) answer than either of these. *See, e.g.*, Dworkin, *supra* note 4, at 317–38, 361–69.

of my own (at least no global, unified theory that can be reduced to a sound bite) defining precisely how the task of textual interpretation *should* proceed. It may be said that it is easier to criticize than to create; that one can't beat even a bad theory with *no* theory; and that inasmuch as I have offered (and rethought) plenty of specific interpretations over the years, it's about time that I roll *my* legal universe into a ball and toss it into the ring as my candidate for what the final rules of the interpretive game must be.

For now, and perhaps permanently, I would respectfully decline that invitation. Indeed, I am doubtful that any defensible set of ultimate "rules" exists. Insights and perspectives, yes; rules, no. But my readily confessed inability to propose a "how to" manual for the interpretive enterprise should not be confused with an inability, or a reluctance, to advance arguments of a "how *not* to" variety, as I have done above and will proceed to do in more detail in what follows. As I trust will become clear (if it is not already), I certainly do *not* regard the Constitution as something that "grows and changes" by some mystical kind of organic, morphing process of the sort Justice Scalia mocks.[15] Nor do I regard the Constitution as something whose occasionally surprising new implications (say, the implication that official segregation by law is unconstitutional, or that laws banning early abortion are unconstitutional) actually represent nothing new at all but, as Professor Dworkin would have it, are all merely inferences that emerge by a straightforward (if sometimes intricate) process of reasoning our way to the right answers to questions of principle that we can be sure the Constitution's authors and/or ratifiers actually put to us ages ago.[16] The process of identifying the meaning of constitutional text seems

---

[15] Scalia, "Common-Law Courts in a Civil-Law System," p. 38. *But see* notes 53–57 and accompanying text, *infra*.

[16] I refer here to Professor Dworkin's reply to Justice Scalia; his extraordinary book *Law's Empire, supra* note 4, stakes out a far more subtle position, which I make no attempt to address in this essay.

to me far more complex and varied than either of these pictures even begins to describe.

To clarify where else I part company with Justice Scalia in particular, I would like to say a few words about one of the principal justifications for our shared belief in the primacy of text when one is construing *federal statutes*. If an Act of Congress would be deemed to mean X but for some body of extratextual evidence adduced to show that one or more lawmakers in the House or Senate hoped, expected, assumed, or feared that the enacted text would instead achieve Y, then giving binding legal effect to that body of evidence so as to *transmute* X into Y would, in a fairly strong sense, circumvent the only process by which, under Article I of the United States Constitution, federal legislation may be enacted. It is for this reason that, in writing from time to time about what I have seen as the misguided enterprise of seeking to decipher the sounds of congressional silence,[17] I have grounded my objections more in the Constitution's structures for national lawmaking than in more general epistemological observations, or in the proposition, which seems to me fairly dubious despite its evident appeal to Justice Scalia,[18] that a judge purporting to rely on "legislative intent" is more likely to impose his or her own will in the name of obedience to law than is a judge purporting to rely on the supposedly "plain meaning" of a given text, or a judge claiming to follow the "original meaning" of that text.

When one is instead undertaking to construe not a federal statute but the United States Constitution, the reasons for rejecting a search for the subjective intent of various framers or ratifiers as the proper mode of interpretation (even their "intent" in Professor Dworkin's sense of what they meant to be saying) are necessarily more complex. For Article I may be thought to fur-

---

[17] *See* Laurence H. Tribe, *Toward a Syntax of the Unsaid: Construing the Sounds of Congressional and Constitutional Silence*, 57 Ind. L.J. 513 (1982); Laurence H. Tribe, *Constitutional Choices* 29–44 (1985).

[18] Based on Justice Scalia's verbal reply to his respondents on the occasion of his Tanner Lectures, March 1995. Hereafter referred to as Tanner reply.

nish an authoritative rejoinder—within a universe that accepts the United States Constitution as providing the decisive rule of recognition for the legality of subconstitutional exercises of governmental power—to the *statutory* interpreter who would have us substitute unexpressed and unenacted thoughts for whatever text actually passed through the fires of bicameral approval and presentment to the president for signature or veto.[19] But there is nothing that can furnish a similarly authoritative rejoinder to the *constitutional* interpreter who would have us make a parallel move with respect to reading, or understanding, something in the United States Constitution itself.

As to provisions of the Constitution that the Continental Congress sent to the states in 1787 for ratification in accord with Article VII of the Constitution drafted in Philadelphia, that Constitution itself tells us at most that ratification by nine of the thirteen states shall suffice for the "establishment of this Constitution" among the states "so ratifying," but it does *not* tell us—and in an important sense it could not possibly tell us— what precisely *counts* as ratification; how one is to understand precisely *what was ratified*; or why, exactly, one should regard ratification in accord with Article VII, which certainly did not comply with the amendment procedure set forth in the then-applicable Articles of Confederation, as either necessary or sufficient to make the text so ratified into what Article VI self-referentially proclaims to be "the supreme Law of the Land."[20]

Similarly, as to constitutional amendments proposed and ratified in accord with Article V of the Constitution, the Constitution tells us at most that amendments ratified by that method "shall be valid to all Intents and Purposes, as part of this

---

[19] *See* U.S. Const. art. I, 1 (bicameralism); *id.*, art. I, 7 (presentment).

[20] Article XIII of the Articles of Confederation required that "any alteration" receive the unanimous consent of the state legislatures. Articles of Confederation and Perpetual Union art. XIII. Article VII of the Constitution, in contrast, provides that "[t]he Ratification of the Conventions of nine States, shall be sufficient for the Establishment of this Constitution between the States so ratifying the Same." U.S. Const. art. VII.

Constitution."[21] But the Constitution does not tell us, and again it could not tell us in any genuinely decisive and authoritative way, exactly what constitutes the *content* of an "amendment" proposed by Congress or by an Article V Convention and ratified by an Article V–approved procedure. There is, it seems to me, no conclusive way to argue that Article V, or anything else in the Constitution, decisively establishes, say, that it is the text and the text alone of something like the First Amendment or the Fourteenth Amendment that has become the "supreme Law of the Land" upon ratification; or that it is solely the "original meaning" of such a provision (either in the Scalia sense *or* in the Dworkin sense) that has been made supreme law by the ratification process; or that it is instead some other cluster of words, ideas, and understandings that is "constitutionalized" by ratification. In choosing among these views of what counts as "the Constitution," and as binding constitutional law, one must of necessity look outside the Constitution itself.

Prominent among the reasons for this perhaps distressing conclusion is the simple but ultimately deep problem of self-referential regress whenever one seeks to validate, from within any text's four corners, a particular method of giving that text meaning.[22] Even if one sought to "prove" a proposition as seem-

---

[21] *See* U.S. Const. art. V. As I have argued elsewhere in response to Professors Bruce Ackerman and Akhil Amar, Article V should also be understood to tell us that amendments put in place by any other method are *not* similarly "valid . . . as Part of this Constitution." *See* Laurence H. Tribe, *Taking Text and Structure Seriously: Reflections on Free-Form Method in Constitutional Interpretation*, 108 Harv. L. Rev. 1221 (1995).

[22] This brings to mind the tale (originally attributable, I believe, to Bertrand Russell) of "turtles all the way down." In one version of the turtle story, a student asserts, following a lecture on the foundations of the universe, that "the universe actually rests on the back of a giant turtle." "But what does the turtle stand on?" asks the professor. "Another, much larger turtle," the student responds. "And what does that turtle stand on?" "Oh, it's turtles all the way down." *See* Roger C. Cramton, *Demystifying Legal Scholarship*, 75 Geo. L.J. 1, 1–2 (1986). On the problem of infinite regress, see Douglas R. Hofstadter, *Gödel, Escher, Bach* 20–21 (1979) (presenting several classic puzzles of self-reference).

ingly straightforward as that the marks on the pages of a given text should be understood as written in *English* rather than in some other tongue or in some obscure code, one could never hope to do so by quoting from the written page itself, whether or not supplemented by aids to translation to which the written page might refer. Even a sentence saying something like "this text is to be read with the aid of the *Oxford English Dictionary*" might, after all, mean something quite different from what most of those who read this essay would take such a sentence to mean—unless one assumes the very thing to be demonstrated about the rules of interpretation to be followed in deciphering the document in question.

Although I nonetheless share with Justice Scalia the belief that the Constitution's written text has primacy and must be deemed the ultimate point of departure; that nothing irreconcilable with the text can properly be considered part of the Constitution; and that some parts of the Constitution cannot plausibly be open to significantly different interpretations, I do not claim these to be rigorously demonstrable conclusions, or confuse them with universally held views.[23] There is certainly nothing in the text itself that proclaims the Constitution's text to be the sole or ultimate point of reference—and, even if there were, such a self-

---

[23] For example, Article III requires criminal trials to be held "in the State where the said Crimes shall have been committed." U.S. Const. art. III, 2, cl. 3. This requirement appears on its face to be structural, part of the very architecture of the Constitution, and thus not waivable by either the defendant or the government. Yet recently the defendants in the Oklahoma bombing case successfully moved to change the venue of their trial from Oklahoma to Colorado. The district judge concluded that "[t]he interests of the victims in being able to attend this trial in Oklahoma are outweighed by the court's obligation to assure that the trial be conducted with fundamental fairness." *A Trial Moves to Denver*, Washington Post, February 22, 1996, at A24. *See also* Thomas C. Grey, *Do We Have an Unwritten Constitution?*, 27 Stan. L. Rev. 703 (1975) (arguing that apart from the Constitution's text there is an unwritten constitution implicit in precedent, practice, and conventional morality). For a discussion and criticism of similar efforts to go beyond the meaning of the amendment procedure set forth in Article V, see Tribe, *supra* note 21.

referential proclamation would raise the problem of infinite regress[24] and would, in addition, leave unanswered the very question with which we began: how is the text's *meaning* to be ascertained?

The Constitution does contain one provision that does indeed serve as a direct instruction to readers about how they are to construe the document. That provision is the Ninth Amendment, which famously asserts, "The enumeration in the Constitution, of certain rights, shall not be construed to deny or disparage others retained by the people."[25] The inherently limited

---

[24] Contrast this with the courts' treatment of commercial contracts proclaiming that the text encompasses the entire agreement. *See, e.g.*, Baxter Healthcare Corp. v. O.R. Concepts, Inc., 69 F.3d 785, 790–91 (7th Cir. 1995) (concluding that if the contract purports on its face to be a complete expression of the whole agreement, it is presumed to supersede all prior discussions and agreements between the parties); Executive Leasing Corp. v. Banco Popular De Puerto Rico, 48 F.3d 66, 69 (1st Cir. 1995) (rejecting extrinsic evidence where the agreement stated that it constituted the entire agreement among the parties). Reading such integration clauses as decisive avoids the self-reference puzzle only because the authoritative nature of these clauses is thought to follow not from the contracts in which they appear but from the background contract law governing those documents. *Cf.* Ogden v. Saunders, 25 U.S. 213 (1827) ("obligation of contracts" protected from state legislative abridgment by Article I, 10, cl. 1, is grounded in positive law of the state itself).

[25] U.S. Const. amend. IX. The only other constitutional provision giving instruction in *how to construe the Constitution* is the Eleventh Amendment, which directs that "[t]he Judicial power of the United States shall not be construed to extend to any suit in law or equity, commenced or prosecuted against one of the United States by Citizens of another State, or by Citizens or Subjects of any Foreign State." In Chisholm v. Georgia, 2 U.S. 419 (1793), the Supreme Court had held that, simply because suits "between a State and Citizens of another State" were included in Article III's enumeration of "controversies" to which "the judicial Power of the United States . . . shall extend," it followed that states automatically lost all otherwise applicable immunities from suit whenever out-of-state citizens sued those states in federal court. That was an extravagant reading of Article III, unwarranted by its text or structure. The Eleventh Amendment was written so as to reverse that dubious construction of Article III, thereby restoring the pre-Chisholm understanding of the article. *See* Tribe, *supra* note 8, 3-26, at 185. Despite what I had thought were compelling argu-

force of any such internal instruction should be manifest even to someone who is not fully familiar with the many lively controversies about just who are the addressees of this instruction (federal officials only, or state officials as well?); about what would count as an action "to deny or disparage" various rights; about whether the "rights" noted include federal constitutional rights or only state-created rights enforced at the option of state authorities;[26] and about whether the rights "retained" should be understood as a closed set fixed as of 1791 (the date of the amendment's ratification) or as an open set whose membership might expand in accord with various interpretive principles.[27]

Thus when Justice Scalia insists of the First Amendment's provision that "Congress shall make no law . . . abridging the freedom of speech" that it ought to be read as a still-photo

---

ments that the Eleventh Amendment, being *only* a rule of construction for Article III, cannot operate to limit Congress's lawmaking powers under, e.g., Article I, *see id.* at 186–87, a closely divided Supreme Court in Seminole Tribe of Florida v. Florida, 1996 WL 134309 (No. 94-12, Mar. 27, 1996), with Justice Scalia joining the majority, quite remarkably treated the Eleventh Amendment as embodying an independent substantive limit on *congressional* power. *See* 1996 WL 134309, at *14. The Court, in my view, failed to respond adequately to Justice Souter's masterful dissent, which elaborately demolished the majority's reasons for holding "for the first time since the founding of the Republic that Congress has no authority to subject a State to the jurisdiction of a federal court at the behest of an individual asserting a federal right." *Id.* at *30 (Souter, J., dissenting).

[26] For the view, apparently held by Justice Scalia, that the Ninth Amendment refers only to rights that are created and enforced by the states, see Calvin R. Massey, *Federalism and Fundamental Rights: The Ninth Amendment*, 38 Hastings L.J. 305 (1987). *But see* John H. Ely, *Democracy and Distrust* 38 (1980) (arguing that the Ninth Amendment "was intended to signal the existence of federal constitutional rights beyond those specifically enumerated in the Constitution").

[27] Justice Scalia joined the four-justice dissent of Justice Thomas in U.S. Term Limits, Inc. v. Thornton, 115 S. Ct. 1842 (1995), construing the parallel Tenth Amendment phrase *"reserved* to the States, respectively, or to the people," as describing an open, indefinitely expandable set. *See id.* at 1878 (Thomas, J., dissenting).

command that Congress not abridge such speech rights of Englishmen as were then extant,[28] I can only marvel at his confidence that he has captured the correct—to use his locution, the "original"—meaning of that majestic guarantee. It seems remarkable, to say the least, that anyone would suppose Americans still fairly fresh from their break with the Crown—1776 was, after all, not ancient history in 1791—truly meant simply to codify the fairly limited freedoms that either their English cousins across the Atlantic, or they and their fellow colonists here, took for granted. What constitutional provision or instruction does Justice Scalia believe requires, or even supports, any such supposition?[29]

This is not to say that the diametrically opposed Dworkinian reading of the same words as self-evidently intended to enact a broad moral principle is demonstrable either. Although I too read the First Amendment's text to embody a set of moral and political principles about the freedom of expression,[30] I cannot bring myself to insist either that the words can bear no other interpretation or that I know mine to be the dominant understanding among whatever category of persons in 1791 might be thought to count as determinative in a suitable theory of original meaning.

When Justice Scalia has voted to strike down state and federal laws against flag burning;[31] to invalidate ordinances that single

[28] Tanner reply.

[29] The rights of Englishmen were, of course, closely constrained. For example, in 1791 it remained a crime to "compass" or imagine the king's death, *see* William T. Mayton, *Seditious Libel and the Lost Guarantee of a Freedom of Expression*, 84 Colum. L. Rev. 101–2 (1984), and, in any event, *no* rights were deemed to be entrenched against Parliament, which was deemed supreme, *see* J.G.A. Pocock, *1776: The Revolution against Parliament, in Three British Revolutions: 1641, 1688, 1776*, at 265 (J.G.A. Pocock ed. 1980); Dickinson, *The Eighteenth-Century Debate on the Sovereignty of Parliament*, 26 Royal Hist. Soc'y, Transactions 189 (1976).

[30] *See* Tribe, *supra* note 8, at 12–1.

[31] *See* Texas v. Johnson, 491 U.S. 397 (1989); United States v. Eichman, 496 U.S. 310 (1990).

out particular acts of cross burning for special punishment based on the racist views those acts express;[32] and to strike down laws that single out for punishment particular killings of animals based on whether those killings are parts of a religious ritual,[33] I have taken comfort from the thought that despite what he has *said* in these lectures about his understanding of the First Amendment as freezing a fixed set of rights into constitutional ice in accord with a supposed "original meaning" of that provision, he has in fact been guided by a conception of the First Amendment more like my own—namely, a conception that embodies not simply a faded snapshot of a bygone age, but instead a set of principles whose understanding may evolve over time, reflecting from the outset at least some of the aspirations of the former colonists about what sorts of rights they and their posterity would come to enjoy against their own government. I have, in other words, taken comfort from the belief that despite what he says, Justice Scalia has not interpreted the freedom of speech as a mere codification of the memories (or perhaps the "memories," mixing hope and desire with actual recollection) of those colonists about what rights they believed had been secure as of a certain moment in the late eighteenth century.[34]

Justice Scalia says that although I might mean that surmise as a compliment, he must decline the honor.[35] He could perhaps claim that if in 1791 laws of the sort he has voted to strike down under the First Amendment, either directly or as somehow applied against the states through the Due Process Clause of the Fourteenth Amendment, had been passed, they would have been invalid because they would have opposed that period's

---

[32] *See* R.A.V. v. City of St. Paul, 112 S. Ct. 2538 (1992).

[33] *See* Church of the Lukumi Babalu Aye, Inc. v. City of Hialeah, 113 S. Ct. 2217 (1993).

[34] *See generally* Dworkin, *supra* note 4; Ronald Dworkin, *A Matter of Principle* (1986); *cf.* Wolf v. Colorado, 338 U.S. 25, 27 (1949) (constitutional rights "do not become petrified as of any one time").

[35] Tanner reply.

understanding of the freedom of speech and the freedom of religion. But any such claim would be incredible. Were the Alien
and Sedition Acts of 1798 contrary to that understanding? Perhaps they were, and perhaps they weren't. Justice Scalia may
claim to know the answer; I don't.[36] But surely the extension of
"freedom of speech" to encompass flag burning or cross burning, or to include anything like the contemporary theory that
content-based and especially viewpoint-based proscriptions of
conduct are constitutionally suspect, would—to a Scalia originalist—entail a most ambitious exercise in attributing modern
ideas of the free speech principle to our predecessors.

That Justice Scalia, despite his protestations, implicitly accepts
some notion of evolving constitutional principles is apparent
from his application of the doctrine of *stare decisis*.[37] Most originalists are willing to accept some version of that doctrine,[38] and
Justice Scalia is no exception, notwithstanding his withering
criticism of a number of precedents, including those construing
the Due Process Clause of the Fourteenth Amendment to have
substantive content. Thus Justice Scalia has implicitly relied on
stare decisis in acknowledging that substantive and not only procedural provisions of the Bill of Rights can be enforced against
the states through the Fourteenth Amendment's Due Process
Clause, even though the Bill of Rights, when ratified in 1791,
was understood to apply only to the federal government, and
even though the Due Process Clause, when ratified in 1868, was
not understood to incorporate the Bill of Rights against the

[36] Adams and Jefferson could more easily agree on the propriety of the First
Amendment than on the constitutionality of the Alien and Sedition Acts of
1798. For background on the controversy surrounding the acts, see J. Smith,
Freedom's Fetters: The Alien and Sedition Laws and American Civil Liberties (1956).

[37] *See* Jed Rubenfeld, *Reading the Constitution as Spoken*, 104 Yale L.J. 1119,
1178–79 (1995) (observing that the doctrine of *stare decisis* reflects the "tempo-
ral extension" element of "written constitutionalism").

[38] *See, e.g.*, Henry Monaghan, *Stare Decisis and Constitutional Adjudication*, 88
Colum. L. Rev. 723 (1988).

states.[39] Justice Scalia asserts that his assumption of the power to invoke *stare decisis* or not to do so does not leave him open to the charge of importing his own views and values into his method of interpretation, because he follows "rules" as to when the disregard of *stare decisis* is appropriate.[40] But even if we assume that Justice Scalia has such "rules" for the selective invocation of *stare decisis*, and for whether to uphold some but not all erroneous decisions of the Supreme Court,[41] what is the origin of those rules? They certainly are not derived from the "original meaning" of the text of the Constitution, as Justice Scalia's interpretive methodology would require.

At the very least, if one is to take constitutional texts as seriously as both Justice Scalia and I say we mean to take them, one ought to draw several basic distinctions in terms of the kind of text one is attempting to construe. Most fundamentally, a text that has a strong transtemporal extension cannot be read in the same way as, say, a statute or regulation enacted at a given

---

[39] *See* TXO Production Corp. v. Alliance Resources Corp., 113 S. Ct. 2711, 2726 (Scalia, J., concurring in the judgment) (accepting "the proposition that the Due Process Clause of the Fourteenth Amendment, despite its textual limitation to procedure, incorporates certain substantive guarantees specified in the Bill of Rights").

[40] Tanner reply.

[41] *See* Planned Parenthood of Southeastern Pennsylvania v. Casey, 505 U.S. 833, 999 (1992) (Scalia, J., concurring in part and dissenting in part) (determining whether Roe v. Wade should be overturned by asking whether that decision, though erroneous, had "succeeded in producing a settled body of law"). During his confirmation hearings, Justice Scalia revealed that his decision whether to overrule precedent he viewed as wrong would be based in part on how woven the "mistake" was into the fabric of the law. A key factor in making this determination would be how long the precedent has existed. For example, he noted that almost no revelation could induce him to overrule Marbury v. Madison, but he would be more willing to overrule a less established case, such as Roe v. Wade. See 13 Roy M. Mersky & J. Myron Jacobstein, *The Supreme Court of the United States: Hearings and Reports on Successful and Unsuccessful Nominations of Supreme Court Justices by the Senate Judiciary Committee, 1916–1986,* at 131–32.

moment in time to deal with a specific problem.[42] As Professor Jed Rubenfeld has reminded us in a provocative article,[43] much of the Constitution simply cannot be understood as a law enacted by a particular body of persons on a specific date but must instead be comprehended as law promulgated in the name of a "people"[44] who span the generations. Perhaps the most dramatic example is the Twenty-Seventh Amendment, proposed and sent to the states in 1789 and finally ratified in 1992.[45]

But we need not look exclusively at provisions ratified long after their original proposal. The First Amendment will suffice to make the point despite its fairly rapid ratification (less than two years after it was proposed to the states).[46] For most of the cases applying the freedoms of speech, press, and religion embodied in the First Amendment enforce those freedoms against the states and necessarily rest on the Fourteenth Amendment, ratified seventy-seven years later in 1868. Those cases apply these freedoms by relying on the Fourteenth Amendment clause forbidding the states to deprive any person of "liberty" "with-

[42] See generally Christopher L. Eisgruber, *The Fourteenth Amendment's Constitution*, 69 S. Cal. L. Rev. 47 (1995); Rubenfeld, *supra* note 38. As Eisgruber and Rubenfeld point out, attempts to analogize the Constitution to a statute enacted at a given moment founder on the fact that statutes assume a backdrop of constitutional norms for determining their legality and construction. Likewise, attempts to analogize the Constitution to a contract proposed by the Convention and accepted by the states fails because the construction and enforcement of contracts presumes the surrounding context of a common-law background within a framework of positive enactments that are in turn grounded in the Constitution.

[43] See Rubenfeld, *supra* note 38, at 1160.

[44] See U.S. Const. pmbl. ("We the People, in order to form a more perfect union. . . .").

[45] See generally Richard B. Bernstein, *The Sleeper Wakes: The History and Legacy of the Twenty-Seventh Amendment*, 61 Fordham L. Rev. 497 (1992). On the ratification process for the Twenty-Seventh Amendment, see Laurence H. Tribe, *The 27th Amendment Joins the Constitution*, Wall St. J., May 13, 1992, at A15.

[46] The First Amendment was presented to the states for ratification on September 24, 1789, and was ratified on December 15, 1791. See George Anastaplo, *The Constitutionalist: Notes on the First Amendment* 209–13 (1971).

out due process of law."[47] Whatever the linguistic difficulties of understanding that phrase to incorporate any substantive limits at all on the content of the rules that state governments are free to promulgate[48]—and whatever the prospects for incorporating the freedoms of speech, press, and religion against the states through the Privileges or Immunities Clause[49] or through the Equal Protection Clause,[50] rather than through the Due Process Clause—it seems to me quite impossible to sustain the proposition that understandings or meanings frozen circa 1791 can possibly serve as the definitive limits to these freedoms as enforced

[47] U.S. Const. amend. XIV.

[48] *See* Tribe, *supra* note 21, at 1297 n.247 (expressing doubts about the doctrine of substantive due process and suggesting that other provisions in the Constitution—particularly the Privileges or Immunities Clause of the Fourteenth Amendment—might be better sources for protecting the substantive liberties of individuals); *see also* Ely, *supra* note 26, at 18. Notwithstanding the historical evidence reflecting that the Fourteenth Amendment was probably understood to treat the words "Due Process of Law" as having substantive content, *see* Tribe, *supra* note 21, at 1297 n.247, and notwithstanding his originalist method of interpretation, Justice Scalia rejects the notion of substantive due process. *See* Scalia, "Common-Law Courts in a Civil-Law System," pp. 24–25.

[49] As I have discussed elsewhere, *see* Tribe, *supra* note 21, at 1297 n.247, I believe that the Slaughter-House Cases, 83 U.S. 36 (1872), incorrectly gutted the Privileges or Immunities Clause, which led courts to rely on substantive due process as a basis for safeguarding substantive rights. *See also* David A. J. Richards, *Conscience and the Constitution* 204–32 (1993) (arguing that the Slaughter-House Cases incorrectly interpreted the Privileges or Immunities Clause).

[50] *See* Police Dept. of Chicago v. Mosley, 408 U.S. 92, 95 (1972) (ordinance prohibiting only nonlabor picketing violated the Equal Protection Clause because there was no "appropriate governmental interest" supporting the distinction inasmuch as "the First Amendment means that government has no power to restrict expression because of its message, its ideas, its subject matter, or its content"); Lee v. Weisman, 505 U.S. 577, 616–622 (1992) (Souter, J., concurring) (asserting that government may not favor religion over nonreligion, and recounting Madison's view that endorsement of religion " 'degrades from the equal rank of Citizens all those whose opinions in Religion do not bend to those of the Legislative authority' ").

today, particularly against the states through a provision that became law in 1868.

Nor need the Fourteenth Amendment be directly implicated for the meaning of a provision of the original Constitution, or of the Bill of Rights, to be affected by intervening constitutional developments. For example, even when the Fifth Amendment is enforced directly against Congress rather than against the states through the Fourteenth Amendment, decisions construing the Due Process Clause of the Fourteenth Amendment to have substantive content necessarily inform our understanding of what the Due Process Clause of the Fifth Amendment, after 1868, must mean.[51] In this way, constitutional provisions sometimes acquire new meanings by the very process of formal amendment to other parts of the Constitution, even when the words contained in the provisions at issue remain unchanged and when only surrounding text has been altered. The Constitution is, after all, a *whole* and not just a collection of unconnected *parts*. When an amendment becomes law under Article I, it becomes "valid . . . *as part of this Constitution*" and not as a freestanding clause or command. Accordingly, while avoiding the error I

---

[51] *See, e.g.*, Adarand Constructors, Inc. v. Pena, 115 S. Ct. 2097 (1995) (noting that equal protection analysis is the same under both the Fifth and Fourteenth Amendments); Bolling v. Sharpe, 347 U.S. 497 (1954) (stating that equal protection analysis under the Equal Protection Clause of the Fourteenth Amendment or under the Due Process Clause of the Fifth Amendment was the same). Significantly, the first Supreme Court opinion to consider at length the meaning of Fourteenth Amendment due process held expressly that that clause had the same meaning as did its counterpart in the Fifth Amendment. *See* Hurtado v. California, 110 U.S. 516, 534–35 (1884). Similarly, the enactment of the Fifteenth Amendment, enfranchising former slaves and persons of color, inevitably alters the meaning of the formula in Article I, 2, cl. 3, for apportioning representatives among the states (the infamous "three-fifths" clause). And the enactment of the Nineteenth and Twenty-Sixth Amendments, enfranchising women and eighteen-year-olds respectively, necessarily affects how we understand the voting rights provision in Section 2 of the Fourteenth Amendment, which provides a formula for reducing representation in the House of Representatives for any state that disenfranchises males aged twenty-one or older.

have elsewhere described as "hyper-integration"[52]—the error of attributing to the Constitution as a whole a degree of coherence, and an absence of compromise, that may be false to its character—we must take care, lest we commit the equally grave error of "dis-integration,"[53] to respect the ways in which the Constitution, even as a purely formal matter, is a work in process, a body of law that "We the People" do *not* in fact "ordain and establish"[54] all at once, in the originalist's equivalent of the physicist's big bang.[55] Whether one includes decisional law construing the text as part of the "law" of the Constitution[56] or includes only the text itself as truly binding law, there's no getting around the fact that what we understand as "the Constitution" speaks across the generations, projecting a set of messages undergoing episodic revisions that reverberate backward as well as forward in time.

Beyond this most fundamental point about transtemporality and the consequent incoherence of an insistence on invariably preserving an "original meaning," there is the further point that not all constitutional provisions are of the same sort even at the moment they are launched upon their historic journey. Some are highly specific and concrete;[57] others, considerably less precise and more transparently fluid.[58] Some refer quite pointedly

---

[52] *See* Laurence H. Tribe & Michael C. Dorf, *On Reading the Constitution* 24–30 (1991).

[53] *See id.* at 20.

[54] U.S. Const. pmbl.

[55] *Cf.* Kathleen M. Sullivan, *Dueling Sovereignties: U.S. Term Limits, Inc. v. Thornton*, 109 Harv. L. Rev. 78, 89 (1995).

[56] *See, e.g.*, Monaghan, *supra* note 39, at 724.

[57] *See, e.g.*, U.S. Const. art. I, 2, cl. 1 (members of the House of Representatives to be chosen every second year); *id.* art. II, 1, cl. 5 (president must be at least thirty-five years old). Indeed, much of the Constitution reads as a rather detailed and reasonably unambiguous blueprint for running a government.

[58] Such seemingly open-ended provisions include "equal protection," *see* U.S. Const. amend. XIV; "privileges and immunities," *see id.* art. IV, 2; and "rights . . . retained by the people," *see id.* amend. IX.

to preserving past practices,[59] while others are more plausibly read as statements of aspiration that could well condemn the very practices of those who wrote or ratified the constitutional provisions in question.[60]

When Justice Scalia has equated my reference to "aspirational" provisions with philosophical pronouncements to be found in places like the Declaration of Independence or in the French Declaration of the Rights of Man and of the Citizen,[61] he missed my point by confusing provisions that merely proclaim broad premises or announce overarching objectives—perhaps like those contained in our own Constitution's preamble, or in the preamble to the Second Amendment[62]—with provisions that, while positively enacting rights or freedoms, do so in terms that can most plausibly be understood less as codifying or pinning down particular privileges that the authors or their English cousins already enjoyed, than as insisting on principles that the authors or ratifiers wished to make binding on their representatives into the indefinite future even if extant practices would have to be substantially revised in order to achieve that end.

Justice Scalia thinks that the mingling of concrete and aspirational provisions would be strange,[63] and concludes that the presence of provisions like that in the Seventh Amendment assuring jury trials in suits at common law for more than twenty dollars somehow counts toward reading everything in the Bill

[59] See, e.g., U.S. Const. amend. VII ("In Suits at common law, where the value in controversy shall exceed twenty dollars, the right of trial by jury shall be preserved, and no fact tried by jury, shall be otherwise re-examined in any Court of the United States, than according to the rules of the common law.").

[60] See, e.g., id. amend. XIV.

[61] Tanner reply.

[62] See U.S. Const. pmbl. ("We the people of the United States, in Order to form a more perfect Union, establish Justice, insure domestic Tranquility, provide for the common defence, promote the general Welfare, and secure the Blessings of Liberty to ourselves and our Posterity, do ordain and establish this Constitution for the United States of America."); id. amend. II ("A well regulated Militia, being necessary to the security of a free State. . . .").

[63] Tanner reply.

of Rights, insofar as linguistically possible, as embodying only concrete guarantees of freedoms held under that era's regime.[64] That simply doesn't follow. On the contrary, the almost embarrassing particularity of references like that to twenty dollars serves to underscore the rather more inspiring generality of many of the other provisions of the Bill of Rights, and of many of the remaining amendments. Moreover, even if it would strike some as odd or unexpected to juxtapose provisions of such variety in a single constitution, that can hardly count to one who follows an originalist methodology.

For Justice Scalia, there appears to be a deeper objection than this essentially aesthetic one. For him, aspirational as opposed to concrete content fundamentally conflicts with the primary purpose of constitutional guarantees: to inhibit change by future generations.[65] Let us, for the sake of argument, assume the accuracy of that astonishingly sweeping pronouncement as to the "primary purpose" of a Constitution designed, as Marshall reminded us long ago, to "endure for the ages."[66] Even so, why assume that in order to pin down some fixed set of rights and to secure them against the winds of change, one would have to *limit* oneself to describing rights in highly particularistic, rule-like terms? Why could one not instead *accompany* such rigid descriptions with principles capable of yielding new and unanticipated implications as future generations come better to understand the deepest meaning and structure of those principles? Why not, that is, attribute to the Constitution the project that its text certainly *appears* to embody—namely, that of guaranteeing, at minimum, that a certain core of rights and freedoms thought to be possessed in the era of promulgation or ratification would be preserved inviolate, while simultaneously assuring, beyond and around that fixed core, a periphery within which a rather more capacious elaboration of the rights and freedoms in question would remain possible and indeed likely?

---

[64] *Id.*   [65] *Id.*

[66] McCulloch v. Maryland, 17 U.S. 316, 415 (1819).

Justice Scalia's principal answer, it seems, is that there must be compatibility between one's interpretation of constitutional guarantees and one's stance concerning the designated instrumentality of enforcement,[67] and that, insofar as the relevant instrumentality for us is judges and courts, this counts decisively against an expansive, evolutionary, principle-like reading of any constitutional guarantee—and decisively in favor of a restrictive, static, and rule-like reading of each guarantee— because a legislature or plebiscite, not judges and courts, constitutes the appropriate interpreter and mouthpiece for the aspirations of its age.[68] Several points seem worth making in response. First, it puts the cart before the horse to insist upon reading constitutional phrases as meaning no more than the judiciary, with its undoubted institutional limitations in a constitutional republic, can be trusted reliably to discern and enforce. As I have urged elsewhere,[69] inasmuch as the Constitution should be understood to address all who are oath-bound to adhere to it,[70] what the Constitution *means* ought to be discussed first, and how much of that meaning life-tenured judges ought to feel free to *impose* and in what circumstances ought to be analyzed afterward. Second, in speaking of "aspirational" provisions of the Constitution, I have not been talking about whatever aspirations succeeding generations might entertain;[71] I have had in

---

[67] Tanner reply.   [68] *Id.*

[69] *See* Tribe, *supra* note 8, 16–20, at 1512–13 (discussing underenforced norms); Laurence H. Tribe, *American Constitutional Law*, 5–12 to 5–15 (1978). *See also* Lawrence Gene Sager, *Fair Measure: The Legal Status of Underenforced Constitutional Norms*, 91 Harv. L. Rev. 1212 (1978).

[70] *See* Paul Brest, *The Conscientious Legislator's Guide to Constitutional Interpretation*, 27 Stan. L. Rev. 585, 587 (1975) (legislators have a duty to "determine, as best they can, the constitutionality of proposed legislation"); Tribe, *supra* note 8, at 1–7, 1–9, 5–1, 16–20 (observing that federal judges are not the only officials sworn to uphold the Constitution, and that their oath requires legislators to heed the Constitution over the views of their constituents).

[71] *See* sources cited in note 34, *supra*. I do not believe that the Constitution is wholly indeterminate and open-ended and, despite suggestions to the contrary, *see* Henry P. Monaghan, *Our Perfect Constitution*, 56 N.Y.U. L. Rev. 343,

mind the rather more confined notion of provisions that are written and understood, sometimes from the outset, to impose requirements or prohibitions that even their authors or ratifiers might occasionally honor in the breach rather than in the observance[72]—mandates, in fact, that few would mistake for mere descriptions or codifications of then-current practice.

Believing that the First Amendment should be regarded as a provision of this sort, I am particularly intrigued to see how Justice Scalia's quite different understanding of its character casts a shadow not only over his reading of the First Amendment itself but also over his understanding of congressional enactments that my interpretation of the First Amendment would lead me

---

356 (1981); Philip Bobbitt, *Constitutional Interpretation* 124 (1991) (stating that I advocate "ratify[ing] a particular decision by subsuming one's instincts for justice within the forms of constitutional argument"), I have never supposed that the Constitution, which at any given time reflects various compromises, should be equated with the ideal form of government. On the contrary, I share the concerns expressed by Robin L. West, *Constitutional Skepticism*, 72 B.U. L. Rev. 765 (1992), about the degree to which equating the Constitution with one's idealized conception of the moral principles that ought to constrain public power in a just society may blind one to the flaws in that document and might deflect energies of political reform into litigation efforts that are either disingenuous or futile or both.

[72] *See, e.g.,* Lee v. Weisman, 505 U.S. 577, 611–16, 616 n.3 (1992) (Souter, J., concurring) (discussing the Framers' understanding of the Establishment Clause, and acknowledging that President Jefferson might have occasionally endorsed religion, notwithstanding his general belief in the unconstitutionality of doing so); Brown v. Board of Educ., 347 U.S. 483, 489–92 (1954) (construing the Fourteenth Amendment to forbid racial segregation of public schools despite the Amendment's "inconclusive" history). *But see* Michael McConnell, *Originalism and the Desegregation Decisions*, 81 Va. L. Rev. 947 (1995) (presenting an originalist defense of *Brown* that attacks the conventional wisdom that the authors and especially the ratifiers of the Fourteenth Amendment assumed racial segregation to be consistent with "equal protection of the laws"). For a critique of Professor McConnell's thesis, see Michael J. Klarman, *Brown, Originalism, and Constitutional Theory: A Response to Professor McConnell*, 81 Va. L. Rev. 1881 (1995); *see also* Laurence H. Tribe, *How Relevant Is "Original Intent" Doctrine?* Legal Times, December 22, 1986, at 12, col. 1.

to read differently. Consider Justice Scalia's discussion of the Supreme Court's 1892 decision in *Church of the Holy Trinity* v. *United States*,[73] in which the Court held that a particular church could not be punished for having encouraged an Englishman to come to New York to serve as its pastor. Congress had exempted from its statutory ban on immigration under contract "professional actors, artists, lecturers, [and] singers."[74] Justice Scalia excoriates the Court for insisting that Congress could not have intended to ban such immigration by pastors.[75] To my eyes, although the *Holy Trinity* Court might well be faulted for pinning its conclusion to a supposition about what Congress must have had in mind, its conclusion makes eminent sense in light of the First Amendment, against whose background the statute had to be construed. If Congress had said, in so many words, that "secular lecturers are exempt, but those whose lectures take the form of religious sermons are subject to the ban," would that not have constituted an abridgment of the freedom of speech and of the free exercise of religion—and perhaps also an establishment of religion—in violation of the First Amendment? Understood as stating a principle against content-based censorship and a mandate of governmental neutrality with respect to religion, the First Amendment would have condemned so discriminatory a federal enactment. Understood instead as an attempt to pin down the rights enjoyed by Englishmen as of 1791, the First Amendment would presumably have meant far less in this context,[76] especially since Parliament clearly would have been free to enact the law in question without violating the "unwritten" British constitution.

Justice Scalia's rejoinder is that one need not decide the constitutional question in order to criticize *Church of the Holy Trinity*, inasmuch as "holding a provision unconstitutional is

---

[73] 143 U.S. 457 (1892).　　　　　　[74] *Id.* at 458–59.

[75] Scalia, "Common-Law Courts in a Civil-Law System." pp. 18–21.

[76] Indeed, Justice Scalia suggests as much, though without quite stating it. *See id.*, p. 20 n.22.

quite different from holding that it says what it does not."[77] True enough. But what, precisely, does the provision in question *say*? *Must* it be read to say, lest violence be done to language, that pastors are not among the "artists" and "lecturers" covered by the exemption? The answer is not to be found by searching legislative history, Justice Scalia and I both appear to believe. Should the answer not be found through elaboration of the text's meaning in light of surrounding context and constitutional principle? And should that method not be even more clearly applicable in dealing with at least such constitutional provisions as the freedom of speech clause in the First Amendment?

I would readily concede that some provisions do not invite, and indeed quite strongly resist, interpretation as broad statements of abstract principle. In particular, as I set forth at greater length elsewhere,[78] those constitutional directives that define— quite literally, *constitute*—a set of governmental institutions and practices, such as the branches of government and their interrelationships, should ordinarily be understood as putting in place a quite definite *architecture* and as specifying the *means* or *instruments* through which power is to be exercised, rather than as proclaiming open-ended *principles* of any kind. Provisions of this sort, even if not as specifically and concretely expressed as, say, the rule that the president must be thirty-five years of age,[79] probably must be taken to have a fixed meaning that it is the task of the faithful interpreter, whether a judge or anyone else, to identify and preserve—unless and until the architecture is changed by constitutional amendment.

[77] *Id.* Similarly, Justice Scalia joined the majority opinion of Chief Justice Rehnquist in Rust v. Sullivan, 500 U.S. 173 (1991) (interpreting Title X of the Public Health Service Act to prohibit use of government funds in programs in which abortion is counseled, and then upholding the statute as so construed under the First Amendment). *But see id.* (O'Connor, J., dissenting) (arguing that the Court should have construed the statute to avoid the serious First Amendment problem that the majority's reading compelled it to resolve).

[78] *See* Tribe, *supra* note 21.   [79] *See* U.S. Const. art. I, 2, cl. 5.

On this view, which I take it Justice Scalia shares, modes of "interpretation" that treat genuinely structural or architectural features of the government created and delimited by the Constitution as themselves merely illustrative, or suggestive, of various ends or purposes are fundamentally illegitimate. But it does not seem to me to be the case, either as a matter of historical fact or as a matter of constitutional logic, that *all* constitutional provisions are of this sort, and it is in this view that I take it Justice Scalia and I will continue to differ. That neither of us has a formula for mechanically deciding which parts of the Constitution *are* purely mechanical, which parts (none, Justice Scalia might insist) state principles that we are bound to elaborate over time, and which combine both characteristics—that there may indeed exist no algorithm for such decisions—may trouble some, and may inspire others, but seems to me, in either event, our inescapable fate.

Comment

☆

MARY ANN GLENDON

As a comparatist with a special interest in contemporary European law, I cannot help but be intrigued by Justice Scalia's use of the "civil-law world" as a metaphor for an American legal environment increasingly dominated by enacted, rather than judge-made, law. For my contribution to this symposium, therefore, I offer some reflections on two questions prompted by the justice's figure of speech: Have civil-law lawyers and judges fared any better than we Americans in the maze of twentieth-century legal materials? If so, what can we learn from their experience?

Comparative analysis can often shed light on a problem by throwing into relief those of our own practices that escape attention just because they are so familiar. Statutory interpretation affords a telling, though embarrassing, example. Film buffs will understand if I put it this way: when it comes to dealing with statutes, we American lawyers are like Igor in the scene from *Young Frankenstein* where Gene Wilder as the doctor says, "Perhaps I could do something about your hump"—and Marty Feldman as Igor replies, "What hump?" For decades, eminent scholars, many of them European trained, have called attention to the primitive state of our skills with legislation. Yet the profession has steadfastly ignored its disability.

Although more than a century has passed since legislative enactments displaced case law as the principal starting points for legal reasoning, we still operate with craft habits formed in an age when, as Roscoe Pound once put it, a lawyer could count on his fingers the statutes with an enduring effect on private‾

95

law.[1] To this day, as Justice Scalia complains, American lawyers' chief technical skills are concerned with court decisions. Most of our fellow citizens, no doubt, would be astonished if they knew how little training the average law student receives in dealing with enacted law, or how completely the profession has neglected the art of legislative drafting (the other side of the coin of interpretation).

As mentioned, some of the leading legal scholars of the twentieth century called attention to these deficiencies—so apparent to anyone familiar with civil law. Pound, for example, wrote:

> [T]he common law has never been at its best in administering justice from written texts. It has an excellent technique of finding the grounds of decision of particular cases in reported decisions of other cases in the past. It has always, in comparison with the civil law, been awkward and none too effective in deciding on the basis of legislative texts.[2]

Karl Llewellyn, even while celebrating the common-law tradition, lamented the "unevenness, the jerkiness" of American work with statutes as contrasted with case law.[3] He added, "It is indeed both sobering and saddening to match our boisterous ways with a statutory text against the watchmaker's delicacy and care of a . . . continental legalcraftsman. . . ."[4] In his own work as a legislative draftsman on the Uniform Commercial Code and other statutes, he relied heavily on German models.

Nevertheless, decades after the New Deal ushered in the era of administrative law, a 1992 Harvard Law School curriculum committee report admitted, "We teach the basic first-year required program almost without regard to the coming of the reg-

---

[1] Roscoe Pound, "The Formative Era of American Law," in *The Life of the Law*, ed. John Honnold (London: Collier-Macmillan, 1964), 59.

[2] *Id.* at 60.

[3] Karl N. Llewellyn, *The Common Law Tradition* (Boston: Little, Brown, 1960), 379.

[4] *Id.* at 380.

ulatory state, and without recognition that statutes and regulations have become the predominant legal sources of our time."[5]
That state of affairs prevails in most American law schools, as
does the practice of teaching advanced statutory courses mainly
through reading court decisions.

What accounts for this persistent deficit? Justice Scalia locates
its origin in professional history. It was judges and practitioners
who took the lead in developing English law, in contrast to continental Europe where the civil law was developed in important
respects by scholars, and was rationalized and systematized at
a crucial stage by comprehensive legislative codifications.[6] In
England and the United States, so long as court decisions were
the principal materials of legal reasoning, common lawyers neither possessed nor required sophisticated skills for interpreting
or drafting enacted law. They had a simple set of tools that were
adequate for dealing with premodern English legislation—statutes which (unlike European codes) typically did not purport to
be complete new sets of authoritative starting points for legal
reasoning.[7] English judges, traditionally, treated such statutes as
a kind of overlay against the background of the common law.
Accordingly, they tried where possible to blend them into the
case law.

The old techniques worked well enough until new forms of
enacted law acquired a prominent and permanent place in the
legal environment. By the mid–twentieth century, however, it
was plain to many observers—Pound,[8] Llewellyn,[9] Cardozo,[10]

---

[5] Report of the Harvard Law School Comprehensive Curricular Assessment
Committee, May 5, 1992, 4 (on file with the author).

[6] See Mary Ann Glendon, Michael Gordon, and Christopher Osakwe, Comparative Legal Traditions (St. Paul, Minn.: West Publishing Co., 1985), 44–54.

[7] See generally Mary Ann Glendon, "Sources of Law in a Changing Legal
Order," 17 Creighton L. Rev. 663 (1983–1984).

[8] Pound, "Common Law and Legislation," 21 Harv. L. Rev. 383 (1908).

[9] Karl N. Llewellyn, The Bramble Bush, 3d ed. (Dobbs Ferry, N.Y.: Oceana,
1960), 78–81. See also Llewellyn, The Common Law Tradition, 379.

[10] Cardozo, " A Ministry of Justice," 35 Harv. L. Rev. 113 (1921).

Landis,[11] Frankfurter[12]—that American lawyers urgently needed to tool up for the modern legal world.

In the 1940s and 1950s, momentum for the study of legislation seemed to be building. This was due in part to the influence of talented New Deal lawyers who had moved from government to law teaching. During the same period, the National Conference of Commissioners on Uniform State Law, the American Bar Association, and the American Law Institute were undertaking ambitious projects to improve and harmonize law, mainly through legislation. A few treatises and teaching materials on statutory interpretation appeared.[13] Hart and Sacks devoted over half of their highly respected 1958 *Legal Process* materials to legislation, administrative law, and the presentation of differentiated techniques for interpreting new, complex types of statutes.[14] Yet the field of legislation remained "a scholarly backwater."[15]

What nipped the emerging serious study of statutes in the bud? Ingrained professional habits and simple inertia are part of the story. But there was also the double whammy of the 1960s and 1970s constitutional rights revolution and the antiregulatory mood of the 1980s. In the heyday of the Warren and Burger Courts, scholarship in statutory fields like tax, securities, and labor law gradually fell out of fashion as constitutional law be-

[11] Landis, "Statutes and the Sources of Law," in *Harvard Legal Essays* (Cambridge: Harvard University Press, 1934), 213.

[12] Frankfurter, "Some Reflections on the Reading of Statutes," 47 *Colum. L. Rev.* 527 (1947).

[13] Reed Dickerson was a pioneer with his books and manuals on legislative drafting and interpretation. *See*, especially, *The Fundamentals of Legal Drafting*, 2d ed. (Boston: Little, Brown, 1986); *The Interpretation and Application of Statutes* (Boston: Little, Brown, 1975).

[14] Henry Hart and Albert Sacks, *The Legal Process: Basic Problems in the Making and Application of Law*, ed. William Eskridge and Philip Frickey (Westbury, N.Y.: Foundation Press, 1994).

[15] Patrick J. Kelley, "Advice from the Consummate Draftsman: Reed Dickerson on Statutory Interpretation," 16 *So. Ill. L.J.* 591, 592 (1992).

came the glamor subject in the legal academy. The legislative process itself came in for disdain as dramatic civil rights decisions promoted the illusion that social change could be effected through litigation. That illusion deflected reformist energy from ordinary democratic politics.[16] Later, advocates of "getting government off our backs" disliked most legislation on principle. Thus, for a variety of reasons, the American legal profession remains disoriented in the "civil-law world."

But was it easier for civil lawyers to find their way as, around the turn of the century, modern legislative creations transformed the world of codes? At first glance, it might seem obvious that they would enjoy a methodological advantage. Historically, the civil- and common-law systems fostered the development of significantly different arrays of professional skills.[17] Just as common lawyers have prided themselves on techniques for dealing with precedent, civil-law lawyers have gloried in their methods for drafting and interpreting codes. No shorthand description can do justice to a praxis, but Winfried Brugger provides a useful summary of the four basic elements of the classical approach: grammatical (sometimes called textual) interpretation, systematic (sometimes called structural)

---

[16] Paul Carrington suggests further reasons why academics have little taste for ordinary politics: "[O]ne must associate with persons who are not always members of an elite. One must go to meetings and not only talk, but also listen politely, often more than once to the same bad idea. One must study and think about issues and problems that are of immediate concern to others, and not only those issues most attractive to one's own interests. . . . To be effective, one must compromise and accommodate. . . . One must risk the sting of visible defeat. . . . [O]ne must sometimes first win trust by bearing the most unwelcome burdens, performing prosaic tasks that do less honor to one's talents than one might wish. . . ." Carrington, "Aftermath," in *Essays for Patrick Atiyah*, ed. P. Cane and J. Stapleton (Oxford: Clarendon Press, 1991), 113, 140.

[17] *Max Weber on Law in Economy and Society*, ed. Max Rheinstein (Cambridge: Harvard University Press, 1954), especially chapter 7. *See also* Max Rheinstein, "Rechtshonoratioren," 34 *RabelsZeitschrift* 1 (1970).

interpretation, historical interpretation, and teleological (sometimes called evolutionary) interpretation.

> In ... grammatical interpretation, philological methods are used to analyze the meaning of a particular word or sentence. In systematic interpretation, one attempts to clarify the meaning of a legal provision by reading it in conjunction with other, related provisions of the same section or title of the legal text, or even other texts within or outside of the given legal system; thus this method relies upon the unity, or at least the consistency, of the legal world. In historical analysis, the interpreter attempts to identify what the founders of a legal document wanted to regulate when they used certain words and sentences. ... In teleological analysis, the [other three elements] are only deemed indicative, not determinative, of the contemporaneous purpose of the legal provision or document.[18]

An extensive civil-law literature testifies that habits and practices based on those methods have proved less helpful in dealing with modern statutes, ordinances, and decrees than with the codes of an earlier day.[19] Traditional interpretive techniques, developed to deal with relatively comprehensive, coherent, self-contained texts, proved difficult to adapt to laws that did not possess the same degree of conceptual and terminological consistency as the great codifications. In consequence, the civil-law systems, like our own, were thrown into interpretive turmoil by new forms of enacted law. Civil-law judges were almost as much at sea as their common-law counterparts when dealing with hastily cobbled statutes shot through with ambiguities and inconsistencies. As new statutes were piled upon older ones, often with an uncertain or overlapping relation to legislation in

[18] Winfried Brugger, "Legal Interpretation, Schools of Jurisprudence, and Anthropology: Some Remarks from a German Point of View," 42 *American Journal of Comparative Law* 395, 396–97 (1994).

[19] Rodolfo Sacco, "La Codification: Forme Dépassée de Legislation?" *Italian National Reports to the XI Int'l Congress of Comparative Law* 65, 67 (Milan: Giuffre, 1982).

other, related, areas, traditional civil-law approaches to interpretation were of less and less assistance.

To put the point another way, civil-law lawyers no longer inhabit a "civil-law world" so far as the materials of legal reasoning are concerned. The term "civil law" connotes, first, private law (property, contracts, torts, family law), and second, the law of the civil codes, which were meant to be complete sets of authoritative starting points for legal reasoning in the private-law fields. Those meanings still have an important place in the legal imagination of civilians, but they lost their centrality in continental European practice long ago.

Just as modern regulatory legislation rivaled the importance of judge-made common law in England and the United States, it challenged the predominance of civil codes in continental Europe. Statutes that removed large areas wholly or partially from the coverage of the codes did reinforce the traditional preeminence of enacted law in civil-law systems, but they diminished the significance of the codes themselves.[20] France, Germany, and the countries whose legal systems are based on theirs thus remain "civil-law" countries only in the sense that their lawyers and judges share a set of habits and practices inherited from a time when the civil code was the heart of the legal system.

To return to the question of comparative advantage, certain features of the civil-law systems did aid their transition to the new statutory and administrative environment. Civil lawyers and judges were at least accustomed to taking their bearings from enacted law, and they were in possession of a high degree of expertise in legislative drafting. All European civil-law countries, furthermore, had long had separate, specialized courts for disputes involving the state and its agencies. And in some countries, separate court systems for tax, social security, and labor law help to maintain coherence in those specialized regulatory areas.

---

[20] *See* Mary Ann Glendon, "The Sources of Law in a Changing Legal Order," 17 *Creighton L. Rev.* 663 (1984).

As in common-law countries, the need to interpret a mounting volume of enacted law obliged civil-law systems to assimilate a huge and expanding body of court decisions. That, in turn, exposed the Achilles heel of civil-law methods: a relative absence of skills in case analysis. Not only has case law been slighted by continental European legal education, but civil-law judges have been slow to develop techniques for the reasoned elaboration of precedent. The French legal system and the many systems modeled on it were especially handicapped by an exceedingly cryptic judicial opinion style. Civil-law systems generally were hobbled by the traditional view of their role as strictly limited to deciding the particular dispute at hand, and by their lack of a formal doctrine of *stare decisis*. That deficit is the civilian counterpart of the common law's weakness with statutes.

Unlike Igor, European jurists have acknowledged their problem. Judges and scholars in Germany were among the first to take measures to develop the skills they lacked. As John P. Dawson wrote in the 1970s, "When the floodtide of caselaw unexpectedly came, German courts and legal scholars proceeded to train each other in developing navigational skills and direction-finding devices...."[21] The French legal profession was slower to adapt, but a 1974 law review article calling for more facts and reasoning in judicial opinions has been influential.[22] Another stimulus is the magisterial comparative study by Swiss scholar Thomas Probst showing that an inadequately developed theory and practice of precedent in his home system had led to a loss of predictability and an unacceptably high frequency of violations of the principle that like cases ought to be treated alike.[23] His conclusions to that effect were based on a compari-

[21] "The General Clauses, Viewed from a Distance," 41 *RabelsZeitschrift* 441, 456 (1977).

[22] Adolphe Touffait and André Tunc, "Pour une motivation plus explicite des décisions de justice notamment celles de la Cour de Cassation," 1974 *Revue trimestrielle du droit civil* 487.

[23] Thomas Probst, *Die Änderung der Rechtsprechung: Eine rechtsvergleichende,*

son of overruling decisions handed down by the United States Supreme Court over a two-hundred-year period with shifts of direction by the Swiss *Bundesgericht* from 1875 to 1990. According to Probst, the traditional dogmatic conception that a single case has no binding effect has adversely affected judicial opinion writing, scholarly case-law analysis, and the integration of case law into the Swiss legal system, with the consequence that similarly situated parties often receive unequal treatment.

Probst therefore called for a rethinking of the role of precedent in the civil-law systems. The time has come, he urged, for civil-law scholars and judges to bring the same level of skill and attention to the study of case law that they have traditionally brought to interpretation of enacted law. In the case of judges, that would require fuller exposure of the grounds for their decisions. He exhorted legal scholars, for their part, to develop methodologies that would help to promote more coherence in judicial practice as well as in the materials of legal reasoning as a whole.

In sum, code-based methods of interpretation seem to have provided the civil-law systems with a modest advantage in dealing with modern statutory law. And, in varying degrees, they are on the way to remedying their long-standing deficiency in case-law skills.

Turning to constitutional interpretation, the example of the German Constitutional Court suggests that the benefits of code-based methods can be even more substantial in the field of constitutional interpretation than in dealing with modern statutes. That example is significant, for the *Bundesverfassungsgericht* has become the most influential tribunal of its kind in the world.

It might be supposed that the United States, with its two-hundred-year-old Constitution, would be far advanced, relative to younger republics, in the theory and practice of constitutional

---

methodologische Untersuchung zum Phänomen der höchsrichterlichen Rechtsprechungsänderung in der Schweiz (civil law) und den Vereinigten Staaten (common law) (Basel: Helbing & Lichtenhahn, 1993).

interpretation. But our Court's first sustained venture in judicial review did not take place until the turn of the twentieth century when a now discredited series of decisions struck down early social legislation. So far as fair criminal procedures, equal legal treatment, free expression, and personal liberties are concerned, the American Supreme Court's experience is comparable to that of its German counterpart—which opened its doors in 1951. In the United States, as in other liberal democracies, the great expansion of constitutional law relating to personal liberties and civil rights has taken place mainly in the half century since World War II ended.

With the era of human rights and constitution making that began in the late 1940s, civil lawyers found themselves on familiar methodological ground. True, the postwar constitutions were novel in the sense that they brought bills of rights and judicial review to several countries for the first time. But the new constitutions resembled the old codes in key respects—in their careful drafting, in their level of generality, in the mutually conditioning relations among their parts, in the presence of several open-ended clauses, and in their aspiration to be enduring. Traditional techniques of code interpretation therefore quickly became the basis of constitutional hermeneutics in continental civil-law systems.

To be sure, consensus on the basics of an approach has not precluded lively controversies over the relative weight to be given to various elements of the method, nor has it resolved the question of how code-based methods are to be supplemented when the text in question is a constitution.[24] The teleological or evolutionary method of construing texts in the light of contemporary circumstances is especially controversial in constitu-

[24] *See* Brugger, "Legal Interpretation"; Dieter Grimm, "Human Rights and Judicial Review in Germany," in *Human Rights and Judicial Review: A Comparative Perspective*, ed. David Beatty (Dordrecht: Nijhoff, 1994), 267; and Donald Kommers, *The Constitutional Jurisprudence of the Federal Republic of Germany* (Durham, N.C.: Duke University Press, 1989), 45–63.

tional law, since the court's "mistakes" cannot be easily corrected. Many European jurists remain nervous about the method's tension with democratic principles, and its potential for abuse.

On the problem of how to adapt traditional methods to the Basic Law of 1949, the views of legal scholar and former Constitutional Court judge Konrad Hesse have been influential. According to Hesse:

> (1) Each interpretation must support the unity of the constitution. (2) In cases of tension or conflict, the principle of practical concordance[25] must be used to harmonize conflicting provisions. (3) All governmental organs must respect the functional differentiation of the constitution, that is, their respective tasks and powers in the separation of powers scheme. (4) Each interpretation must try to create an integrative effect with regard to both the various parties of a constitutional dispute as well as to social and political cohesion. (5) . . . . Each interpretation shall attempt to optimize all the aforementioned elements.[26]

In the decisions of the German Constitutional Court on freedom of speech, election law, church-state relations, personal freedoms, equality, and economic liberties,[27] the influence of the grammatical and systematic methods (what Justice Scalia calls textualism) is strong and unmistakable. The Court has at times been bold in deploying the teleological method, but its boldest decisions, like those of John Marshall, are also among its most prudent. The historical method, in Germany as in other civil-law

[25] According to this principle, tension among constitutional provisions and values must be resolved in such a way as to optimize the scope of each. In other words, the judge must not permit one constitutional value to prevail completely over another.

[26] Summarized by Brugger, "Legal Interpretation," at 398–99.

[27] The leading decisions of the German Constitutional Court have been translated and collected in Kommers, *The Constitutional Jurisprudence of the Federal Republic of Germany.*

systems, appears to be of less importance than the other three approaches.[28]

One of the traits that most conspicuously differentiates the *Bundesverfassungsgericht's* decisions from those of the American Supreme Court also helps to keep teleological interpretation from running wild. That is the practice of attending consistently to the language and structure of the entire Constitution—to the document as a whole, and to the relationship of particular provisions to one another as well as to the overall design for government. (The Court is aided, it should be noted, by the fact that the Basic Law is a more detailed, integrated, and contemporary document than the United States Constitution.)

In the 1930s, Ernst Freund theorized that judicial review, over time, would inevitably subordinate the text and structure of the Constitution to case law.[29] But now that systems of judicial review have been operating for several decades in many liberal democracies, it is apparent that the text and structure need not be thrust so deeply into the background as they have been in the United States. Though recognizing that constitutions are more political and more open-ended than codes, German courts and scholars have found it natural to proceed from close textual analysis in the light of overall structure to consideration of purpose both in the light of history and in the light of circumstances as they exist at the time of decision.[30] The text, however, remains the alpha and omega of interpretation. It serves both as the

[28] In continental practice, the historical method is decreasingly employed as a code or constitution ages. Thus French jurists do not regard the ideas and intentions of the drafters of the Civil Code of 1804 as controlling in present-day cases. Alfred Rieg, "Judicial Interpretation of Written Rules," 40 *La. L. Rev.* 49, 62 (1979). As early as 1977, the German Constitutional Court cited the age of the 1949 Basic Law as a reason for declining to accord decisive weight to evidence of the intent of the framers. *See* Kommers, *The Constitutional Jurisprudence of the Federal Republic of Germany*, 316.

[29] Ernst Freund, "Constitutional Law," in *Encyclopaedia of the Social Sciences* (New York: Macmillan, 1937), 4:248–49.

[30] *See generally* Brugger, "Legal Interpretation."

starting point for judicial reasoning and the outer limit on the range of possible results.

When civil lawyers come to American law schools for graduate work, they often express surprise at the degree to which the case method dominates our approach to courses based on enacted law. In particular, they find it hard to understand why constitutional law courses and materials typically begin, not with a study of the language and design of the Constitution, but with a case (usually *Marbury* v. *Madison*).[31] Their puzzlement deepens as weeks pass and discussion moves from one case to another, with the Constitution itself glimpsed only in a fragmentary way. One visiting German lawyer told me that when a student asked about the role of text in constitutional analysis, an American professor's response was: "Forget about the text!"

There is no mystery about how we arrived at that state of affairs. At the time of the Founding, the American Framers were torn "between a global rejection of any and all methods of constitutional construction and a willingness to interpret the constitutional text in accordance with the common law principles that had been used to construe statutes."[32] In the early years of the republic, that tension was temporarily resolved when a consensus developed on a version of originalism.[33] In the *Lochner* era, however, old habits took over. When American judges had to interpret novel types of legislation, and to review them for conformity to the Constitution, they naturally proceeded in the way they knew best.

Their instinct was to fill gaps or ambiguities in the text (statutory or constitutional) with judge-made common law, rather

---

[31] 5 U.S. (1 Cranch) 137 (1803). It was not always thus. According to Paul Carrington, students in early American law schools were required to have a detailed knowledge of the Constitution, and *The Federalist* was often used as a basic text. Carrington, "Butterfly Effects: The Possibilities of Law Teaching in a Democracy," 41 *Duke L.J.* 741, 759 (1992).

[32] H. Jefferson Powell, "The Original Understanding of Original Intent," 98 *Harv. L. Rev.* 885, 887 (1985).

[33] *Id.*

than to search first, as a civil lawyer would, for guiding principles in the structure and design of the instrument. In *Lochner* v. *New York*[34] and related cases, the Court construed the Constitution in such a way as to harmonize with, rather than displace, a common-law background where protection of property rights and freedom of contract were ensconced at the time as leading principles. As Pound put it, "[The common lawyer] thinks of the constitutional checks upon legislation as enacting common-law limitations, and systematically develops those checks in terms of the common law."[35] Oliver Wendell Holmes Jr. and others protested in vain that the Constitution was not just an overlay on the private law of property and contract.[36]

Even after Holmes's views prevailed in other respects, his methodological point was not fully absorbed. Certainly neither text nor precedent justified the *Lochner* Court in giving property (and freedom of contract to acquire property) the same exalted position in constitutional law that those goods enjoyed in late-nineteenth-century common law. On the other hand, to nearly read property out of the Constitution, as the Court later did in cases involving New Deal legislation and takings, was equally indefensible.

In the 1950s and 1960s, the preference for judge-made over enacted law that had been so evident in constitutional interpretation at the turn of the century came to the fore again as the Supreme Court embarked on a second exciting adventure with judicial review. This time, the Court began treating selected elements of the Bill of Rights as discrete starting points for creative judicial elaboration. Both the Court majority and its academic admirers in that period studiously ignored what a civil-law approach would have kept in view—that the Constitution is not only a charter of rights but a design for government

---

[34] 198 U.S. 45 (1905).

[35] Pound, "Formative Era of American Law," 61.

[36] *See, e.g.*, Lochner v. New York, 198 U.S. 45, 74–76 (1905) (Holmes, J., dissenting); Adkins v. Children's Hospital, 261 U.S. 525, 570 (1923) (Holmes, J., dissenting); Truax v. Corrigan, 257 U.S. 312, 344 (1921) (Holmes, J., dissenting).

which places important limits on both judicial and legislative lawmaking.

As Justice Scalia emphasizes, the Court's freewheeling approach to constitutional interpretation is a far more serious matter than its careless ways with statutes. For as judicial lawmaking expands, the democratic elements in our republican experiment atrophy. American men and women not only are deprived of having a say on how we order our lives together, but we lose the skills of self-government. Something seems to have gone wrong somewhere—as in that fateful scene where Igor accidentally picks up the wrong specimen jar, the one marked, "Beware: Abnormal Brain!"

In 1991, Cass Sunstein ruefully commented in the *New Republic*, "[O]ur understanding of constitutional interpretation remains in a primitive state."[37] From a comparative perspective, it would appear that many of our difficulties arise from the frequent omission of steps that civil lawyers perform instinctively. Consider the Court's religion-clause jurisprudence, which has been described by scholars of all persuasions, and even by the justices themselves, as unprincipled, incoherent, and unworkable. As a matter of judicial craftsmanship, it is dismaying to observe how little intellectual effort the Court devoted in the 1940s to the enormously complex issues created by the effort to make the establishment language of the First Amendment binding on the states. And how can one account for the consistent failure of Court majorities to recognize what grammatical and structural methods make clear: that the religion language of the First Amendment has a context—in the First Amendment as a whole, the Bill of Rights, and the overall constitutional design?[38] Systematic attention to text and structure would not have produced "one right answer" to thorny interpretive problems in the church-state area, but it would have helped to reduce extreme and atextual outcomes.

[37] Cass R. Sunstein, Book Review, *New Republic*, March 11, 1991, 35.

[38] *See* Mary Ann Glendon and Raul Yanes, "Structural Free Exercise," 90 *Mich. L. Rev.* 477 (1991).

At this point, an inquisitive person may be wondering how the civil-law disadvantage in dealing with case law has affected constitutional interpretation. The general language of constitutions, after all, necessarily gives rise to a large body of court decisions. At least where Germany is concerned, Constitutional Court judges have clearly benefited from the experience of an earlier generation of judges on ordinary courts in addressing that problem.[39] In fact, it is difficult to read the German Constitutional Court's decisions without the sense that they stand up better, on the whole, to the traditional criteria by which common lawyers have evaluated judicial work than our own Court's decisions in the same period. The *Bundesverfassungsgericht* displays impressive skill in maintaining principled continuity in the law, explaining the outcomes of particular cases in ways that can make sense even to the losers and others who disagree, and assuring predictability and stability without foreclosing adaptation to changing social and economic circumstances.

That observation leads me to surmise that things here at home may be even worse than Justice Scalia suggests. He is undoubtedly correct as to the historical matter that many of our interpretive ills are due to the survival of common-law habits in the world of enacted law. But it ought to be said that those habits were good ones, even if ill-adapted to statutory and constitutional interpretation. It is cause for concern, therefore, that they seem to be deteriorating. As Justice Scalia himself points out, *stare decisis* is losing vigor. More ominously, subjective forms of judging in which neither text nor precedent is accorded much respect seem increasingly to be accepted as legitimate.[40]

[39] For detailed studies of the developments in private law, *see* John P. Dawson, *The Oracles of the Law* (Ann Arbor: University of Michigan Press, 1968); "Unconscionable Coercion: The German Version," 89 *Harv. L. Rev.* 1041 (1976); and "Judicial Revision of Frustrated Contracts: Germany," 63 *B.U.L. Rev.* 1039 (1983).

[40] *See* Mary Ann Glendon, *A Nation under Lawyers* (New York: Farrar Straus & Giroux, 1994), chapter 8.

As for the Supreme Court, it is not at all clear that it really remains attached to common-law methods—in the sense of attending in each case to providing a fair resolution of the case at hand, mooring that decision in text and tradition, fairly exposing its reasoning processes, and providing guidance to parties in future cases. Often its rulings look less like the reasoned elaboration of principle than like the products of majority vote. At times the Court appears just to be lurching along in irrational and unpredictable fashion, like the monster in the old version of *Frankenstein*. Rather than just being differently abled, American judges and lawyers may be losing the ability to do what they once did best!

Justice Scalia has been more critical of the courts than of the institutions that supposedly exist to nurture and improve legal skills. Yet, as with statutory interpretation, the law schools bear their share of responsibility. Up to about thirty years ago, the typical constitutional law course was heavy on federalism, separation of powers, and the commerce clause, but light on the Bill of Rights. The obvious remedy would have been to teach the whole Constitution from preamble to last amendment—as a design for self-government as well as a charter of rights, and as a text whose parts cannot be understood in isolation from one another. But in the 1960s the emphasis was simply shifted to individual rights. As a result, con law classes have long had the same relation to the Constitution as the Elgin Marbles have to the Parthenon. The student sees the professor's prized collection of fragments, but the well-proportioned structure in which these treasures once had their appropriate place is nowhere on display. The Constitution is like a wonder of another world, an ancient temple once used for activities that are no longer much practiced among us—deliberation, voting, local self-government.

In recent years, a diverse and growing group of scholars have opened debate on the relationship between our system of limited government and the system of rights that has been at the forefront of constitutional theory in recent years. And they are approaching interpretive problems by attending to the overall design of the Constitution and the relationships among its provisions. Without neglecting our rights tradition or the principles embodied in two centuries of precedent, they are attempting to restore separation of powers, federalism, and constitutional text and structure to "a central and appropriate place" in constitutional theory.[41]

Those efforts may well bring about improvement in constitutional law teaching, but it is not likely that chaos in the field of constitutional interpretation will diminish any time soon. For if textualism, structuralism, and originalism advance, it can be predicted that selective deployment of textualism, structuralism, and originalism will advance as well. Judges and scholars who have abandoned the notions of principled judging and objective scholarship will not be easily constrained.

That observation brings me to what, in the end, is probably the most important civil-law advantage in interpretation: a certain legal culture widely shared by lawyers and judges with diverse personal backgrounds, economic views, and political sympathies. As Dawson's studies showed, "predictability and coherence could not have been maintained in German law in such high degree if a close working partnership had not been maintained between a career judiciary and legal scholars, both highly trained in and firmly committed to the same highly ordered system of legal ideas."[42]

So long as the American legal profession lacks even a minimal consensus that judges, practitioners, and scholars have roles and responsibilities to which personal interests and predilections must be subordinated, Americans sharing Justice Scalia's legal values cannot possibly subscribe to the interpretive techniques (especially the wild-card teleological method) that work reason-

[41] Miller, "Rights and Structure in Constitutional Theory," 8 *Soc. Phil. and Pol.* 196, 198 (1991).

[42] Dawson, "The General Clauses," 455.

112

ably well in many parts of the "civil-law world." Our legal culture also explains why many American friends of democratic and rule-of-law values have been driven to espouse what most civil lawyers would regard as excessively rigid forms of textualism. As Dawson put it, "We have much to learn from German law and should be willing to admire the German achievement. It does not follow that we have the means to emulate it."[43]

The subject of democratic values leads me to one last observation. In Justice Scalia's conclusion, he warns that if the public perceives that constitutional interpretation is up for grabs, the Bill of Rights will not long serve to protect important liberties from majority rule. The dreaded "monster" in this part of his story is tyranny of the majority, the same villain as in the tales told by many of the justice's critics.

Tyranny of the majority does sound alarming. It conjures up visions of peasants with their pitchforks storming the scientist's castle. Small wonder that it is a favorite slogan of those who would prefer to forget that one of the most basic American rights is the freedom to govern ourselves and our communities by bargaining, education, persuasion, and, yes, majority vote. But is tyranny of the majority really the greatest danger that faces a country when its courts foreclose ordinary politics in one area after another—and when more and more decision-making power over the details of everyday life is concentrated in large private and public bureaucracies? Which is more likely: that unruly majorities will have their way? Or that the democratic elements in our republican experiment will wither away, while new forms of tyranny by the powerful few arise? Whom should we fear more: an aroused populace, or the vanguard who know better than the people what the people should want?

Tyranny, as Tocqueville warned, need not announce itself with guns and trumpets. It may come softly—so softly that we will barely notice when we become one of those countries where

---

[43] "Unconscionable Coercion: The German Version," 89 *Harv. L. Rev.* 1041, 1126 (1976).

there are no citizens but only subjects. So softly that if a well-meaning foreigner should suggest, "Perhaps you could do something about your oppression," we might look up, puzzled, and ask, "What oppression?"

Comment

☆

RONALD DWORKIN

1

JUSTICE SCALIA has managed to give two lectures about meaning with no reference to Derrida or Gadamer or even the hermeneutic circle, and he has set out with laudable clarity a sensible account of statutory interpretation. These are considerable achievements. But I believe he has seriously misunderstood the implications of his general account for constitutional law, and that his lectures therefore have a schizophrenic character. He begins with a general theory that entails a style of constitutional adjudication which he ends by denouncing.

His initial argument rests on a crucial distinction between law and intention. "Men may intend what they will," he says, "but it is only the laws that they enact which bind us,"[1] and he is scornful of decisions like *Holy Trinity*, in which the Supreme Court, conceding that the "letter" of a statute forbade what the church had done, speculated that Congress did not intend that result. Indeed, he is skeptical about the very idea of a corporate legislative "intention"; most members of Congress, he says, have never thought about the unforeseen issues of interpretation that courts must face. A careless reader might object, however, that any coherent account of statutory interpretation *must* be based on assumptions about someone's (or some body's) intention, and that Scalia's own account accepts this at several points. Scalia admits that courts should remedy "scrivener's error."[2] He rejects "strict constructionism"—he thinks the

---

[1] Scalia, "Common-Law Courts in a Civil-Law System," p. 17.
[2] *Id.* p. 20.

115

Supreme Court's "literalist" decision in the "firearm" case, *Smith* v. *United States*, was silly.[3] He credits at least some of the "canons" of interpretation as being an "indication" of meaning.[4] And he says that it would be absurd to read the First Amendment's protection of speech and press as not applying to handwritten notes, which are, technically, neither.[5]

Each of these clarifications allows respect for intention to trump literal text, and the careless objection I am imagining therefore claims an inconsistency. Scalia's defenders might say, in reply to the objection, that he is not an *extreme* textualist, and that these adjustments are only concessions to common sense and practicality. But that misunderstands the objection, which is that the concessions undermine Scalia's position altogether, because they recognize not only the intelligibility but the priority of legislative intention, both of which he begins by denying. If judges can appeal to a presumed legislative intent to add to the plain meaning of "speech" and "press," or to subtract from the plain meaning of "uses a firearm," why can they not appeal to the same legislative intent to allow a priest to enter the country? Scalia's answer to this objection must not rely on any self-destructive "practicality" claim. It must rely instead on a distinction between *kinds* of intention, a distinction he does not make explicitly, but that must lie at the heart of his theory if the theory is defensible at all.

This is the crucial distinction between what some officials intended to *say* in enacting the language they used, and what they intended—or expected or hoped—would be the *consequence* of their saying it. Suppose a boss tells his manager (without winking) to hire the most qualified applicant for a new job. The boss might think it obvious that his own son, who is an applicant, is the most qualified; indeed he might not have given the instruction unless he was confident that the manager would think so too. Nevertheless, what the boss *said*, and *intended* to say, was that the most qualified applicant should be hired, and if the

---

[3] *Id.* pp. 23–24.   [4] *Id.* p. 27.   [5] *Id.* pp. 37–38.

manager thought some other applicant better qualified, but hired the boss's son to save his own job, he would not be following the standard the boss had intended to lay down.

So what I called the careless objection is wrong. The supposed lapses from Scalia's textualism it cites are not lapses at all, because textualism insists on deference to one kind of intention—semantic intention—and in all his remarks so far cited Scalia is deferring to that. Any reader of anything must attend to semantic intention, because the same sounds or even words can be used with the intention of saying different things. If I tell you (to use Scalia's own example) that I admire bays, you would have to decide whether I intended to say that I admire certain horses or certain bodies of water. Until you had, you would have no idea what I had actually said even though you would know what sounds I had uttered. The phrase "using a firearm" might naturally be used, in some contexts, with the intention of describing only situations in which a gun is used as a threat; the same phrase might be used, in other contexts, to mean using a gun for any purpose including barter. We do not know what Congress actually said, in using a similar phrase, until we have answered the question of what it is reasonable to suppose, in all the circumstances including the rest of the statute, it intended to say in speaking as it did.

When we are trying to decide what someone meant to say, in circumstances like these, we are deciding which clarifying *translation* of his inscriptions is the best. It is a matter of complex and subtle philosophical argument what such translations consist in, and how they are possible—how, for example, we weave assumptions about what the speaker believes and wants, and about what it would be rational for him to believe and want, into decisions about what he meant to say.[6] The difficulties are greatly increased when we are translating not the utterances of a real person but those of an institution like a legislature. We rely on personification—we suppose that the institution has

---

[6] Reference to work of Quine, Grice, and Davidson.

semantic intentions of its own—and it is difficult to understand what sense that makes, or what special standards we should use to discover or construct such intentions. Scalia would not agree with my own opinions about these matters.[7] But we do agree on the importance of the distinction I am emphasizing: between the question of what a legislature intended to say in the laws it enacted, which judges applying those laws must answer, and the question of what the various legislators as individuals expected or hoped the consequences of those laws would be, which is a very different matter.

Holy Trinity illustrates the difference and its importance. There can be no serious doubt that Congress meant to say what the words it used would naturally be understood to say. It is conceivable—perhaps even likely—that most members would have voted for an exception for English priests had the issue been raised. But that is a matter of (counterfactual) expectations, not of semantic intention. The law, as Scalia emphasizes, is what Congress has said, which is fixed by the best interpretation of the language it used, not by what some proportion of its members wanted or expected or assumed would happen, or would have wanted or expected or assumed if they had thought of the case.[8] Not everyone agrees with that judgment. Some lawyers think that it accords better with democracy if judges defer to reasonable assumptions about what most legislators wanted or would have wanted, even when the language they used does not embody those actual or hypothetical wishes. After all, these lawyers argue, legislation should reflect what those who have been elected by the people actually think best for the country. Scalia disagrees with that judgment: he thinks it more democratic to give semantic intention priority over expectation intention when the two conflict, as they putatively did in *Holy Trinity*.

[7] See chapter 9 of my *Law's Empire* (Harvard University Press, 1986).

[8] I am prescinding, as Scalia does, from the question Professor Tribe raises about the constitutionality of the statute considered in *Holy Trinity* if it is read to say what it was plainly intended to say.

2

Now consider the implications of textualism so understood for the most important part of Scalia's judicial duties: interpreting the exceedingly abstract clauses of the Bill of Rights and later rights-bearing amendments. Scalia describes himself as a constitutional "originalist." But the distinction we made allows us a further distinction between two forms of originalism: "semantic" originalism, which insists that the rights-granting clauses be read to say what those who made them intended to say, and "expectation" originalism, which holds that these clauses should be understood to have the consequences that those who made them expected them to have. Consider, to see the difference, the *Brown* question: does the Fourteenth Amendment guarantee of "equal protection of the laws" forbid racial segregation in public schools? We know that the majority of the members of Congress who voted for that amendment did not expect or intend it to have that consequence: they themselves sustained racial segregation in the schools of the District of Columbia.[9] So an expectation-originalist would interpret the Fourteenth Amendment to permit segregation and would declare the Court's decision wrong. But there is no plausible interpretation of what these statesmen meant to *say*, in laying down the language "equal protection of the laws," that entitles us to conclude that they *declared* segregation constitutional. On the contrary, as the Supreme Court held, the best understanding of their semantic intentions supposes that they meant to, and did, lay down a general principle of political morality which (it had become clear by 1954) condemns racial segregation. So, on that ground, a semantic-originalist would concur in the Court's decision.

[9] For a recent account of the literature, see Michael J. Klarman, Brown, *Originalism and Constitutional Theory: A Response to Professor McConnell*, 81 Virginia Law Review, 1881 (1995).

If Scalia were faithful to his textualism, he would be a semantic-originalist. But is he? Notice his brief discussion of whether capital punishment offends the Eighth Amendment's prohibition against "cruel and unusual" punishments. An expectation-originalist would certainly hold that it does not, for the reasons Scalia cites. The "framers" would hardly have bothered to stipulate that "life" may be taken only after due process if they thought that the Eighth Amendment made capital punishment unconstitutional anyway. But the question is far more complicated for a semantic-originalist. For he must choose between two clarifying translations—two different accounts of what the framers intended to *say* in the Eighth Amendment. The first reading supposes that the framers intended to say, by using the words "cruel and unusual," that punishments generally thought cruel at the time they spoke were to be prohibited—that is, that they would have expressed themselves more clearly if they had used the phrase "punishments widely regarded as cruel and unusual at the date of this enactment" in place of the misleading language they actually used. The second reading supposes that they intended to lay down an abstract principle forbidding whatever punishments are in fact cruel and unusual. Of course, if the correct translation is the first version, then capital punishment does not violate the Eighth Amendment. But if the second, principled, translation is a more accurate account of what they intended to say, the question remains open. Just as the manager in my story could only follow his boss's principled instruction by using his own judgment, so judges could then only apply the Eighth Amendment by deciding whether capital punishment is in fact cruel and has now become (as in fact it has become, at least among democracies) unusual.

The textual evidence Scalia cites would be irrelevant for a semantic-originalist who translated the Eighth Amendment in a principled rather than a concrete and dated way. There is no contradiction in the following set of claims. The framers of the Eighth Amendment laid down a principle forbidding whatever punishments are cruel and unusual. They did not themselves expect or intend that that principle would abolish the death penalty, so they provided that death could be inflicted only after due process. But it does not follow that the abstract principle they stated does not, contrary to their own expectation, forbid capital punishment. Suppose some legislature enacts a law forbidding the hunting of animals that are members of "endangered species" and then, later in its term, imposes special license requirements for hunting, among other animals, minks. We would assume that the members who voted for both provisions did not think that minks were endangered. But we would not be justified in concluding from that fact that, as a matter of law, minks were excluded from the ban even if they plainly *were* endangered. The latter inference would be an example of *Holy Trinity* thinking.

You will now understand my concern about Scalia's consistency. For he cites the view that capital punishment is unconstitutional as so obviously preposterous that it is cause for wonder that three justices who served with him actually held such an opinion.[10] If he were an expectation-originalist, we would not be surprised at that view, or at the evidence he offers to support it. But for a semantic-originalist the question just *cannot* be foreclosed by references to the death penalty in the rest of the Constitution. A semantic-originalist would also have to think that the best interpretation of the Eighth Amendment was the dated rather than the principled translation, and even someone who might be drawn to that dated interpretation could not think the principled one *preposterous*.

On the contrary, it is the dated translation that seems bizarre. It is near inconceivable that sophisticated eighteenth-century statesmen, who were familiar with the transparency of ordinary moral language, would have used "cruel" as shorthand for "what we now think cruel." They knew how to be concrete when they intended to be: the various provisions for criminal and civil process in the Fourth, Fifth, Sixth, and Seventh

[10] Scalia, "Common-Law Courts in a Civil-Law System," p. 46.

121

Amendments do not speak of "fair" or "due" or "usual" procedures but lay down very concrete provisions. If they had intended a dated provision, they could and would have written
an explicit one. Of course, we cannot imagine Madison or any of
his contemporaries doing that: they wouldn't think it appropriate to protect what they took to be a fundamental right in such
terms. But that surely means that the dated translation would be
a plain mistranslation.

So Scalia's impatience with what seems the most natural
statement of what the authors of the Eighth Amendment intended to say is puzzling. Part of the explanation may lie in his
fear of what he calls a "morphing" theory of the Constitution—
that the rights-bearing clauses are chameleons which change
their meaning to conform to the needs and spirit of new times.
He calls this chameleon theory "dominant," but it is hardly even
intelligible, and I know of no prominent contemporary judge or
scholar who holds anything like it. True, a metaphorical description of the Constitution as "living" has figured in constitutional rhetoric of the past, but this metaphor is much better understood as endorsing, not the chameleon theory, but the view
I just described as the one that Scalia, if he were a semantic-
originalist, might be expected to hold himself—that key constitutional provisions, as a matter of their original meaning, set out
abstract principles rather than concrete or dated rules. If so, then
the application of these abstract principles to particular cases,
which takes fresh judgment, must be continually reviewed, not
in an attempt to find substitutes for what the Constitution says,
but out of respect for what it says.

I have defended that view in a series of books over the last
decade,[11] and some of what I have written might strike Scalia as
saying that the Constitution itself changes, though I meant the
opposite. I said, for example, that, subject to the constraints of

[11] See chapter 10 of *Law's Empire*, *supra* note 7, chapter 5 of *Life's Dominion*
(Alfred Knopf, 1993), and *Freedom's Law: The Moral Reading of the American Constitution* (Harvard University Press, 1996).

integrity which require judges to keep faith with past decisions, "The Constitution insists that our judges do their best collectively to construct, reinspect, and revise, generation by generation, the skeleton of freedom and equality of concern that its great clauses, in their majestic abstraction, command."[12]

It is that moral and principled reading of the Constitution, not the mythic chameleon claims he describes, that Scalia must produce reasons for rejecting. In his contribution to this volume, Professor Tribe endorses the abstract moral reading of many clauses as well; he proposes that the First Amendment, for example, be read as abstract.[13] So we may gauge Scalia's arguments against the principled reading by studying his response to Tribe's suggestion. Scalia argues that the First Amendment should be read not as abstract but as dated—that it should be read, that is, as guaranteeing only the rights it would have been generally understood to protect when it was enacted. He makes three points: first, that since many parts of the Bill of Rights are plainly concrete—the Third Amendment's prohibition against quartering troops during peacetime, for example— the "framers" probably intended to make them all so; second, that the "framers" would presumably be anxious to insure that their own views about free speech were respected even if later generations no longer agreed; and, third, that in any case the

---

[12] *Life's Dominion, supra* note 11, 145.

[13] I assume that Tribe agrees that some constitutional clauses are semantically principled, though in his lecture he called such clauses "aspirational," a term that is often used to describe ambitions that government should strive to realize as distinct from law it is bound to obey. Many contemporary constitutions, for example, set out "aspirational" declarations of economic and social rights meant to have that function. Scalia may have understood Tribe in that sense in describing Tribe's view of the First Amendment as a *"beau idéal."* Based on Justice Scalia's verbal reply to his respondents on the occasion of the Tanner Lectures, March 1995. Hereafter referred to as Tanner reply. The abstract principles of the Constitution's text are as much law—as much mandatory and as little aspirational or idealized—as any other clauses. See *Freedom's Law, supra* note 11.

"framers" would not have wanted to leave the development of a constitutionalized moral principle to judges.[14]

These are all arguments for ignoring the natural semantic meaning of a text in favor of speculations about the expectations of its authors, and the Scalia of the preconstitutional part of these lectures would have ridiculed those arguments. First, why shouldn't the "framers" have thought that a combination of concrete and abstract rights would best secure the (evidently abstract) goals they set out in the preamble? No other national constitution is written at only one level of abstraction, and there is no reason to suppose the authors of the Bill of Rights would have been tempted by that kind of stylistic homogeneity. Second, as I said, Enlightenment statesmen were very unlikely to think that their own views represented the last word in moral progress. If they really were worried that future generations would protect rights less vigorously than they themselves did, they would have made plain that they intended to create a dated provision. Third, we must distinguish the question of what the Constitution means from the question of which institution has final authority to decide what it means. If, as many commentators think, the "framers" expected judges to have that authority, and if they feared the consequences for abstract rights, they would have taken *special* care to write concrete, dated clauses. If, on the contrary, they did not expect judicial review, then Scalia's third argument fails for that reason. The First Amendment turns out to be his *Holy Trinity*.

He ignores, moreover, an apparently decisive argument against a translation of the First Amendment as dated. There *was* no generally accepted understanding of the right of free speech on which the framers could have based a dated clause even if they had wanted to write one. On the contrary, the disagreement about what that right comprises was much more profound when the amendment was enacted than it is now. When the dominant Federalist party enacted the Sedition Act in 1798,

[14] Tanner reply.

its members argued, relying on Blackstone, that "the freedom of speech" meant only freedom from "prior restraint"—in effect, freedom from an advance prohibition—and did not include any protection at all from punishment *after* publication.[15] The opposing Republicans argued for a dramatically different view of the amendment: as Albert Gallatin (Jefferson's future secretary of the treasury) pointed out, it is "preposterous to say, that to punish a certain act was not an abridgment of the liberty of doing that act." All parties to the debate *assumed* that the First Amendment set out an abstract principle and that fresh judgment would be needed to interpret it. The Federalists relied, not on contemporary practice, which hardly supported their reading,[16] but on the moral authority of Blackstone. The Republicans relied, not on contemporary practice either, but on the logic of freedom. No one supposed that the First Amendment codified some current and settled understanding, and the deep division among them showed that there was no settled understanding to codify.

So Scalia's discussion of the First Amendment is as puzzling as his briefer remarks about the Eighth Amendment. Now consider what he says about the Fourteenth Amendment's guarantee of "equal protection of the laws." He says that that clause "did not, when it was adopted, and hence did not in 1920, guarantee equal access to the ballot but permitted distinctions on the basis not only of age but of property and sex."[17] Why is he so sure that the Equal Protection Clause did not always forbid discrimination on grounds of age, property, or sex (or, for that matter, sexual orientation)? Certainly when the amendment was adopted, few people *thought* that the clause had that consequence, any more than they thought that it had the consequence

[15] For a recent description of the arguments over the Sedition Act, see Anthony Lewis, *Make No Law* (Random House, 1991), chapter 7.

[16] See the exchange of views between Professors Leonard Levy and David Anderson, summarized in the former's 1985 edition of his book, *Legacy of Suppression*.

[17] Scalia, "Common-Law Courts in a Civil-Law System," p. 47.

of making school segregation illegal. But the semantic-original-ist would dismiss this as just what the framers and later genera-tions of lawyers expected, not a matter of what the framers actu-ally *said*. If we look at the text they wrote, we see no distinction between racial discrimination and any other form of discrimina-tion: the language is perfectly general, abstract, and principled. Scalia now reads into that language limitations that the lan-guage not only does not suggest but cannot bear, and he tries to justify this mistranslation by attributing understandings and ex-pectations to statesmen that they may well have had, but that left no mark on the text they wrote. The Equal Protection Clause, we might say, is Scalia's *Holy Trinity* cubed.

What has happened? Why does the resolute text-reader, dic-tionary-minder, expectation-scorner of the beginning of these lectures change his mind when he comes to the most fundamen-tal American statute of them all? He offers, in his final pages, an intriguing answer. He sees, correctly, that if we read the abstract clauses of the Bill of Rights as they were written—if we read them to say what their authors intended them to say rather than to deliver the consequences they expected them to have—then judges must treat these clauses as enacting abstract moral prin-ciples and must therefore exercise moral judgment in deciding what they *really* require. That does not mean ignoring precedent or textual or historical integrity or morphing the Constitution. It means, on the contrary, enforcing it in accordance with its text, in the only way that this can be done. Many conservative judges therefore reject semantic originalism as undemocratic; elected judges, they say, should not have that responsibility. Scalia gives nearly the opposite reason: he says the moral reading gives the people not too little but too much power, because it politicizes the appointment of Supreme Court justices and makes it more likely that justices will be appointed who reflect the changing moods of the majority. He fears that the constitu-tional rights of individuals will suffer.

History disagrees. Justices whose methods seem closest to the moral reading of the Constitution have been champions, not en-

126

emies, of individual rights, and, as the political defeat of Robert Bork's nomination taught us, the people seem content not only with the moral reading but with its individualist implications. Scalia is worried about the decline of what he believes to be property rights embedded in the Constitution but ignored in recent decades. He reminds liberals that rights of criminal defendants may also be at risk. But even if we were persuaded that the Court has gone too far in neglecting property rights, and also that *Maryland* v. *Craig* compromised a valid constitutional right, these assumed mistakes would hardly outweigh the advantages to individual freedom that have flowed from judges' treatment of the great clauses as abstract.

It is, however, revealing that this is the scale on which Scalia finally wants his arguments to be weighed, and it may provide a final explanation, if not justification, for the inconsistency of his lectures as a whole. His most basic argument for textualism is drawn from majoritarian theory: he says that it is undemocratic when a statute is interpreted other than in accordance with the public text that was before legislators when they voted and is available to everyone in the community afterwards. His most basic argument for rejecting textualism in constitutional interpretation, on the other hand, reflects his *reservations* about majority rule. As with most of us, Scalia's attitudes about democracy are complex and ambivalent. I disagree with his judgment about which individual rights are genuine and important, and about whether the moral reading is a threat or an encouragement to freedom. But I agree with him that in the end the magnet of political morality is the strongest force in jurisprudence. The power of that magnet is nowhere more evident than in the rise and fall of his own love affair with textual fidelity.

Response

☆

ANTONIN SCALIA

A FEW WORDS are appropriate in response to the statements of the commenters. The length of my response to each bears no relationship, either direct or inverse, to my estimation of the value the statement in question has brought to this discussion—which for all four is great indeed. Some, however, require me to explain myself more than others.

PROFESSOR WOOD

In Professor Wood's scholarly presentation, the principal point with which I take issue is his assertion that in the English legal system statutes "had to make sense in terms of the rest of the common law," i.e., that there was an inherent judicial power to ignore statutory law. Professor Wood accepts as orthodoxy Lord Chief Justice Coke's statement in Dr. Bonham's case (1610) that "in many cases, the common law will controul Acts of Parliament and sometimes adjudge them to be utterly void: for when an Act of Parliament is against common right and reason, or repugnant, or impossible to be performed, the common law will controul it and adjudge such Act to be void."[1] It was not orthodoxy at all, but an extravagant assertion of judicial power, scantily supported by the authorities cited,[2] vehemently criticized by contemporaries,[3] and seemingly abandoned by Coke

---

[1] Dr. Bonham's Case, 8 Co. Rep. 114a, 118a, 77 Eng. Rep. 646, 652 (K.B. 1610).

[2] *See* Theodore F. T. Plucknett, *Bonham's Case and Judicial Review*, 40 Harv. L. Rev. 30, 35–48 (1926).

[3] *Id.* at 49–52.

himself in his *Institutes*.[4] As Professor J. H. Baker describes it, "[l]ittle more was heard in England of judicial review of statutes, and Coke's doctrine of 1610 was whittled down into a presumption to be applied only where a statute was ambiguous or in need of qualification by necessary implication."[5] The genuine orthodoxy is set forth in Blackstone:

> I know it is generally laid down more largely, that acts of parliament contrary to reason are void. But if the parliament will positively enact a thing to be done which is unreasonable, I know of no power that can control it: and the examples usually alleged in support of this sense of the rule do none of them prove, that where the main object of a statute is unreasonable the judges are at liberty to reject it; for that were to set the judicial power above that of the legislature, which would be subversive of all government.[6]

The record does not, I think, support Professor Wood's belief that Blackstone was setting forth a new, eighteenth-century doctrine, spawned by "the emergence . . . of the idea of parliamentary sovereignty and the positivist conception of law." Blackstone was not new; Dr. Bonham's case was eccentric. I agree with Profesor Wood's contention that English judges claimed "to have the capacity to interpret and construe parliamentary statutes in such a way as to fit them into the entire legal structure." My essay acknowledges (and indeed insists) that modern American judges have the same capacity (see pp. 16–17). But construing statutory ambiguities to be harmonious with the common law is quite different from ignoring plain texts that contradict the "right and reason" of the common law.

The quotation from Blackstone suggests another point on

[4] Edward Coke, *The Fourth Part of the Institutes of the Laws of England* 37, 41 (photo. reprint 1979) (London: M. Flesher 1628). *See also* J. H. Baker, *An Introduction to English Legal History* 242 (3d ed. 1990).

[5] Baker, *supra* note 4, at 242.

[6] 1 William Blackstone, *Commentaries on the Laws of England* 91 (photo. reprint 1979) (1765).

which I disagree with Professor Wood. From the premise that "[t]he sharp distinction we recognize between legislation and adjudication is a modern one," he concludes that "there are very good deeply rooted historical reasons why statutory construction in both England and America has involved a good deal of judicial common-law type interpretation." I am sure what he means by his premise is not that the inherent difference between legislation and adjudication has been recognized only in modern times (Aristotle saw it quite clearly);[7] but rather that appreciation of the desirability of *separating* the adjudicative function from the legislative one is a modern development (modern, that is, as historians rather than journalists use the term, whereby Montesquieu is modern). I suppose that is correct. In this country, colonial legislatures often sat as courts and rendered their decrees in laws.[8] But while legislatures regularly adjudicated, I am not aware of any evidence that adjudicative tribunals (the Supreme Judicial Court of Massachusetts, for example, as opposed to the General Court, which is its legislature) felt free to legislate—that is, to change or depart from statutory law in the course of promulgating their adjudicative degrees. To the contrary, it was accepted (Lord Chief Justice Coke in Dr. Bonham's case notwithstanding) that courts were in principle bound by statutory enactments.

This is not to say that I take issue with Professor Wood's conclusion that the problem of judicial rewriting of democratically adopted texts is "deeply rooted in our history" and that "judges have exercised that sort of presumably undemocratic authority from the very beginning." To acknowledge that is simply to acknowledge that there have always been, as there undoubtedly always will be, willful judges who bend the law to their wishes. But acknowledging evil is one thing, and embracing it is something else. It seems to me that Professor Wood neglects that

[7] *See* Aristotle, *Nichomachean Ethics*, in 2 *The Complete Works of Aristotle* 1795–96 (Jonathan Barnes ed., 1984).

[8] See the discussion of this point in Plaut v. Spendthrift Farm, Inc., 115 S.Ct. 1447, 1453–56 (1995).

distinction when he surmises that "the enhanced judicial discretion and judicial lawmaking of the past three or four decades represents a change in degree, not one in kind." There has been a change in kind, I think, not just in degree, when the willful judge no longer has to go about his business in the dark—when it is publicly proclaimed, and taught in the law schools, that judges *ought* to make the statutes and the Constitution say what they think best.

Professor Wood thinks that textualism, as I have described it, is "as permissive and as open to arbitrary judicial discretion and expansion as the use of legislative intent or other interpretative methods, if the text-minded judge is so inclined." I do not agree. No textualist-originalist interpretation that passes the laugh test could, for example, extract from the United States Constitution the prohibition of capital punishment that three nontextualist justices have discovered, or the prohibition of abortion laws that a majority of the Court has found. Moreover, the judge who uses "legislative intent or other interpretative methods" does not entirely abandon text, but rather adds to whatever manipulability text contains the (much greater) manipulability of his extratextual methodology. I concede, of course, that textualism is no ironclad protection against the judge who wishes to impose his will, but it is *some* protection. The criterion of "legislative intent," by contrast, positively invites the judge to impose his will; by setting him off in search of what does not exist (there is almost never any genuine legislative intent on the narrow point at issue), it reduces him to guessing that the legislature intended what was most reasonable, which ordinarily coincides with what the judge himself thinks best. Other nontextual methodologies are similarly wish-fulfilling.

Finally, I may respond to Professor Wood's disheartening perception that what I have addressed—the proclivity of our judges to function like legislators—is, after all, "only an aspect of the problem that we Americans have with our judges, possibly more a manifestation of the problem than a cause of it." Every issue, I suppose, is "only an aspect" of some other one—

132

the problem we Americans have with our judges, for example, being only an aspect of the problem we Americans have with our government, which in turn is only an aspect of the problem we Americans have with life. But whether life-tenured judges are free to revise statutes and constitutions adopted by the people and their representatives is not merely—as Professor Wood describes it—a question of some "importance," but a question utterly central to the existence of democratic government. Professor Wood is perhaps correct that the problem I have discussed is only a "manifestation" of a more fundamental ill; again, most things are. But whereas I do not know whether that more fundamental ill is treatable (or indeed even what it is), I am sure that we can induce judges, as we have induced presidents and generals, to stay within their proper governmental sphere.

PROFESSOR TRIBE

My principal response to Professor Tribe is that he perceives more of an agreement between us regarding the methodology of interpreting a legal text than I think exists. He is correct that we both regard as irrelevant the intentions of the drafters; but he regards as irrelevant, as well, the understandings of those to whom the text is promulgated, except to the very limited extent of ascertaining "the linguistic frame of reference." What he means by that, as I understand him, is that once we assure ourselves that the English word "speech" in the eighteenth century meant pretty much what it means today, that is all the guidance we need take from the society which embraced the guarantee of "the freedom of speech" in 1791. Thereafter, the phrase "the freedom of speech" careens down through the centuries, to produce whatever results later Americans desire it to produce, so long as those results have something to do with the ability to engage in "speech"—or, as Professor Tribe more kindly (but no less frighteningly) describes the process, the phrase is "launched

133

upon a historic voyage of interpretation in which succeeding generations . . . would elaborate what the text means in ways all but certain not to remain static."

Elsewhere in his essay, Professor Tribe describes these roaming provisions as designed to "reflect[] . . . the *aspirations* of the former colonists about what sorts of rights they and their posterity *would come to enjoy* against their own government" (emphasis added). I do not believe that. If you want aspirations, you can read the Declaration of Independence, with its pronouncement that "all men are created equal" with "unalienable Rights" that include "Life, Liberty and the pursuit of Happiness." Or you can read the French Declaration of the Rights of Man and of the Citizen, adopted two years before our Bill of Rights, which says that "[m]en are born and remain free and equal in their rights,"[9] that "[l]iberty consists of being able to do whatever does not harm another,"[10] and that "[t]he law has the right to proscribe only those acts harmful to society."[11] There is no such philosophizing in our Constitution, which, unlike the Declaration of Independence and the Declaration of the Rights of Man, is a practical and pragmatic charter of government. The aspirations of those who adopted it are set forth in its prologue—"to insure domestic Tranquility," among other things, and "to secure the Blessings of Liberty to ourselves and our Posterity." The operative provisions of the document, on the other hand, including the Bill of Rights, abound in concrete and specific dispositions. In addition to those described earlier, see, for example, the Third Amendment ("[n]o Soldier shall, in time of peace be quartered in any house, without the consent of the Owner"), the Fourth Amendment ("no Warrants shall issue, but upon probable cause, supported by Oath or affirmation, and particularly describing the place to be searched, and the persons or things to be seized"), and the Seventh Amendment ("[i]n Suits at common law, where the value in controversy shall exceed twenty dollars, the right of trial by jury shall be preserved").

[9] Declaration of the Rights of Man and of the Citizen (August 26, 1789), Art. 1, translated in 10 *The New Encyclopaedia Britannica* 71 (15th ed. 1985).

[10] *Id.*, Art. 4.   [11] *Id.*, Art. 5.

To be sure, in addition to these unquestionably nonaspirational provisions, there are others that in isolation may or may not be regarded as aspirational, such as the provision of the First Amendment that "Congress shall make no law . . . abridging the freedom of speech." One might read the phrase "the freedom of speech," as Professor Tribe chooses to, as the statement of a *beau idéal*—a lofty principle as indeterminate as "all men are created equal," the precise content of which is, as he describes it, "capable of elaboration and application only through the processes of moral philosophy." Alternatively, one might understand "the freedom of speech" that was not to be "abridged" to be the then extant speech rights of Englishmen. Professor Tribe contends that I have no basis for choosing between these two interpretations, since there is no "constitutional provision or instruction" (other than the limited provision of the Ninth Amendment) specifying how the document is to be construed. But documents rarely specify how they are to be construed—which does not mean that there is no right and no wrong construction. The principal determinant of meaning is context, which in this case negates an aspirational interpretation.

It would be most peculiar for aspirational provisions to be interspersed randomly among the very concrete and hence obviously nonaspirational prescriptions that the Bill of Rights contains—"jury trials in suits at common law for more than twenty dollars," followed by "all men are created equal," followed by "no quartering of troops in homes." It is more reasonable to think that the provisions are all of a sort. Professor Tribe emphasizes that such provisions as the guarantees of "the freedom of speech" and of "due process of law" are abstract and general rather than specific and concrete; but abstraction and generality do not equate with aspiration. The context suggests that the abstract and general terms, like the concrete and particular ones, are meant to nail down current rights, rather than aspire after future ones—that they are abstract and general references to *extant* rights and freedoms possessed under the then-current regime. The same conclusion follows from the evident purpose of the provisions. To guarantee that the freedom of speech will be

135

no less than it is today is to guarantee something permanent; to guarantee that it will be no less than the aspirations of the future is to guarantee nothing in particular at all.

An additional consideration is this: If Professor Tribe is correct that the Bill of Rights is aspirational, then Chief Justice Marshall was wrong in establishing the courts as its ultimate interpreter. The perception underlying the holding of *Marbury* v. *Madison* is that judges are naturally appropriate expositors of the law—that "[i]t is emphatically the province and duty of the judicial department to say what the law is."[12] Judges are *not*, however, naturally appropriate expositors of the aspirations of a particular age; that task can be better done by legislature or by plebiscite. In other words, if the guarantees of the Bill of Rights had been aspirational, their textually unassigned implementation should, like the implementation of the French Declaration of the Rights of Man, have been left to the legislature.

Of course under Professor Tribe's methodology not *all* provisions of the Constitution are aspirational—not *all* are, as he says, "generative of constitutional principles broader or deeper than their specific terms might at first suggest." (The "right to bear arms," I suspect, is limited to musketry in the National Guard.)[13]

___

[12] Marbury v. Madison, 5 U.S. (1 Cranch) 137, 177 (1803). In other words, Marbury v. Madison presumes the bringing "of the higher law of the Constitution within the realm of ordinary law," as discussed by Professor Wood, *supra* p. 62.

[13] Professor Tribe regards the Second Amendment's prologue ("A well regulated Militia, being necessary to the security of a free State") as a textual obstacle to my interpretation of the Second Amendment as a guarantee that the federal government will not interfere with the individual's right to bear arms for self-defense. This reading of the text has several flaws: It assumes that "Militia" refers to "a select group of citizen-soldiers," Joyce Lee Malcolm, *To Keep and Bear Arms* 136 (1994), rather than, as the Virginia Bill of Rights of June 1776 defined it, "the body of the people, trained to arms," see *id.*, at 148. (This was also the conception of "militia" entertained by James Madison, who, in arguing that it would provide a ready defense of liberty against the standing army that the proposed Constitution allowed, described the militia as "amounting to near half a million of citizens with arms in their hands." *The Federalist* No. 46, at 322 (Jacob E. Cooke ed., 1961).) The latter meaning makes the prologue of

When the question arises, as it must in any reader's mind, *which* provisions embark "upon a historic voyage of interpretation" and which stay at home—and the further question, what determines the *direction* of those that wander—Professor Tribe takes refuge in "candor and ... self-conscious humility." Rejecting base "certitude," he acknowledges that he does not know the answer to either of these questions. Indeed, he is not even sure there *are* any answers—only "insights and perspectives." I do not mean to disparage candor and humility, virtues that are not only admirable but also rare, particularly in intellectual circles. They would assuredly carry the day if the issue before us were quality of character, rather than soundness of interpretive theory. But they are of little use to the judge who must determine whether and whither the Constitution has wandered, and who is not permitted to render a candid and humble judgment of "Undecided."

At this point in his commentary, Professor Tribe inserts a parenthetical exercise in deconstructing the Constitution. It is rational, he says, to take the position that federal statutes mean

---

the Second Amendment commensurate with the categorical guarantee that follows ("the right of the people to keep and bear Arms, shall not be infringed"); the former produces a guarantee that goes far beyond its stated purpose—rather like saying "police officers being necessary to law and order, the right of the people to carry handguns shall not be infringed." It would also be strange to find in the midst of a catalog of the rights of *individuals* a provision securing *to the states* the right to maintain a designated "Militia." Dispassionate scholarship suggests quite strongly that the right of the people to keep and bear arms meant just that. In addition to the excellent study by Ms. Malcolm (who is not a member of the Michigan Militia, but an Englishwoman), see William Van Alstyne, *The Second Amendment and the Personal Right to Arms*, 43 Duke L.J. 1236 (1994). It is very likely that modern Americans no longer look contemptuously, as Madison did, upon the governments of Europe that "are afraid to trust the people with arms," *The Federalist* No. 46; and the traveling Constitution that Professor Tribe espouses will probably give effect to that new sentiment by effectively eliminating the Second Amendment. But there is no need to deceive ourselves as to what the original Second Amendment said and meant. Of course, properly understood, it is no limitation upon arms control by the states.

only what they say, and cannot have their meaning changed by extratextual evidence, because any other disposition would "circumvent the only process by which, under Article I of the United States Constitution, federal legislation may be enacted." But, he points out, there is not (and cannot possibly be) anything in the Constitution which demonstrates that *the Constitution* means only what it says. There is a fallacy in this contrast: one cannot rely upon a meaningless Constitution to give substance to statutes enacted under it. If we cannot be sure that the Constitution means only what it says, we cannot be sure that federal statutes can only be enacted through the process of Article I. Deconstruction is fun. It is also quite useless for those who want to get on with the business of living and acting in the real world. Professor Tribe evidently agrees, since at the conclusion of this digression he acknowledges (in a sort of *credo quia absurdum est*) that he "nonetheless," and without reason, believes "that the Constitution's written text has primacy and must be deemed the ultimate point of departure." I am willing to accept that grudging acknowledgment and move on.

I must respond to Professor Tribe's contention that, since I have "voted to strike down state and federal laws against flag burning; to invalidate ordinances that single out particular acts of cross burning for special punishment based on the racist views those acts express; and to strike down laws that single out for punishment particular killings of animals based on whether those killings are parts of a religious ritual," I am at heart an aspirationist. He means it as a compliment, but I must decline the honor. All three of the examples he selects involve the First Amendment, for which the Court has developed long-standing and well-accepted principles (not out of accord with the general practices of our people, whether or not they were constitutionally required as an original matter) that are effectively irreversible. That my opinions sought to apply those principles faithfully does not prove, as Professor Tribe suggests, that I am unfaithful to my interpretive philosophy. Originalism, like any other theory of interpretation put into practice in an ongoing system of law, must accommodate the doctrine of *stare decisis*; it cannot remake the world anew. It is of no more consequence at this point whether the Alien and Sedition Acts of 1798 were in accord with the original understanding of the First Amendment than it is whether *Marbury* v. *Madison* was decided correctly. Where originalism will make a difference is not in the rolling back of accepted old principles of constitutional law but in the rejection of usurpatious new ones. My fidelity to the methodology should be judged, not by the First Amendment cases Professor Tribe selects, but (to speak of decisions handed down only this past term) by cases discovering a novel constitutional right against statewide laws denying special protection to homosexuals,[14] a novel constitutional right against excessive jury awards,[15] a novel constitutional right against being excluded from government contracts because of party affiliation,[16] a novel constitutional prohibition of single-sex state schools,[17] and a novel constitutional approval of federal appellate review of jury verdicts.[18]

Professor Tribe appears to believe that there is something uniquely inappropriate about the acceptance of *stare decisis* by an originalist. Surely not. The whole function of the doctrine is to make us say that what is false under proper analysis must nonetheless be held to be true, all in the interest of stability. It is a compromise of all philosophies of interpretation, his no less than mine. The demand that originalists alone "be true to their lights" and forswear *stare decisis* is essentially a demand that they alone render their methodology so disruptive of the established state of things that it will be useful only as an academic exercise and not as a workable prescription for judicial governance. Professor Tribe says that my assumption of the power to

[14] Romer v. Evans, 116 S. Ct. 1620 (1996).

[15] BMW of North America v. Gore, 116 S. Ct. 1589 (1996).

[16] Board of County Comm'rs, Wabaunsee Cty. v. Umbehr, 116 S. Ct 2342 (1996); O'Hare Truck Serv., Inc. v. City of Northlake, 116 S. Ct. 2353 (1996).

[17] United States v. Virginia, 116 S. Ct. 2264 (1996).

[18] Gasperini v. Center for Humanities, Inc., 116 S. Ct. 2211 (1996).

invoke, or not invoke, *stare decisis* leaves me "open to the charge of importing [my] own views and values" into the law, which my mode of interpretation was supposed to guard against. I cannot deny that *stare decisis* affords some opportunity for arbitrariness—though I attempt to constrain my own use of the doctrine by consistent rules.[19] In any event, I have never claimed that originalism inoculates against willfulness; only that (unlike aspirationism) it does not cater to it. And finally, Professor Tribe's concern over the fact that whatever rules I use for *stare decisis* are not to be found in the original meaning of the Constitution is simply inexplicable. As I have explained, *stare decisis* is not *part of* my originalist philosophy; it is a pragmatic *exception* to it.

Professor Tribe argues that "a text that has a strong transtemporal extension cannot be read in the same way as, say, a statute or regulation enacted at a given moment in time to deal with a specific problem." I entirely agree with that, and indeed made the same point at the outset of my discussion of constitutional interpretation. But reading it in a different way does not require reading it in such fashion that its meaning *changes*. It is simply a caricature of originalism to portray it as narrow and hidebound—as ascribing to the Constitution a listing of rights "in highly particularistic, rule-like terms." I take many things to be embraced within "the freedom of speech," for example, that were not in fact protected, because they did not exist, in 1791—movies, radio, television, and computers, to mention only a few. The originalist must often seek to apply that earlier age's understanding of the various freedoms to new laws, and to new phenomena, that did not exist at the time. That is a difficult task (though not as difficult as intuiting, or perhaps prescribing, soci-

---

[19] *See, e.g.*, BMW of North America, Inc. v. Gore, 116 S. Ct. 1589, 1610 (1996) (Scalia, J., dissenting); Planned Parenthood v. Casey, 505 U.S. 833, 993 (1992) (Scalia, J., concurring in judgment in part and dissenting in part); Walton v. Arizona, 497 U.S. 639, 672–73 (1990) (Scalia, J., concurring in part and concurring in judgment).

ety's evolving aspirations)—which explains why originalists do not have ready answers to all questions and sometimes disagree among themselves.[20] But giving the Constitution what Professor Tribe calls "transtemporal extension" in *that* fashion is quite different from saying that it has no constant meaning, so that the *very acts* that were perfectly constitutional in 1791 (political patronage in government employment and contracting, for example) may be *un*constitutional today.

It is impossible to disagree with Professor Tribe's statement that "constitutional provisions sometimes acquire new meanings by the very process of formal amendment to other parts of the Constitution." The first ten amendments, for example, certainly caused the federal powers conferred by the original body of the document to be more limited than they originally were. That is standard textual construction. But Professor Tribe means something more mystic than that, whereby, by virtue of the mere existence and use of the amendment process, "what we understand as 'the Constitution' speaks across the generations, projecting a set of messages undergoing episodic revisions that reverberate backward as well as forward in time." It seems to me that the existence and use of an amendment process is not something that sets the Constitution apart from other democratically adopted texts, but rather something that it has in common with them; amended statutes do not reverberate backward and forward any more than the text of the amendments requires. If the Constitution, intended to be a more permanent document, should be treated at all differently insofar as amendments are concerned, one would think that, if anything, the normal rule of construction that repeals by implication are disfavored[21] would be *more rigorously* applied. I am at a loss to confront Professor Tribe's point more specifically, since the only example he provides is the Fourteenth Amendment, and the only reverberating

[20] Compare my opinion with that of Justice Thomas in McIntyre v. Ohio Elections Comm'n, 115 S. Ct. 1511 (1995).

[21] *See* Posadas v. National City Bank, 296 U.S. 497, 503–05 (1936).

effect he alludes to is produced not by the text of that Amendment but by the holding of subsequent *case law* that the Due Process Clause extends the Bill of Rights to the states. If the *text* of the Fourteenth Amendment said that "the Bill of Rights, which has hitherto been a restriction only upon the federal government, shall henceforth be a restriction also upon the states," there might be room for an argument that the 1868 *understanding* of the Bill of Rights was thereby adopted, not only for the states but for the federal government as well. But it does not say that, and that is in any event not the argument Professor Tribe is making, since he no more wants to enshrine the values of 1868 than he does those of 1791; he wants the Constitution to travel all the way to the values of 1996, which leaves him almost a century and a half still to traverse. The notion of the amendment process as establishing a Constitution which "project[s] a set of messages undergoing episodic revisions that reverberate backward as well as forward" seems to me a desperate attempt to give some hint of textual legitimacy to the vagrant Constitution. There is little use in having a written constitution if textual construction is so indistinguishable from poetry.

To end on a happy note, I would like to welcome Professor Tribe into the company of those who have "doubts about the doctrine of substantive due process," though my joy at this conversion must be tempered by disappointment—nay, foreboding—at his simultaneous announcement that henceforth provisions of the Constitution *other than* the Due Process Clause will serve as the instruments of his aspiring. Professor Tribe's doubts regarding substantive due process, elaborated more fully in a law-review article cited in his footnote, rest upon his conclusion that, even though "any state legislature voting to ratify" the Fourteenth Amendment "would have understood [the Due Process Clause] as having substantive as well as procedural content," the "basic linguistic point" that "substantive due process [is] an oxymoron . . . has great force."[22] Alas, even when we

---

[22] Laurence H. Tribe, *Taking Text and Structure Seriously: Reflections on Free-*

come to agree in result, Professor Tribe's methodology and mine are poles apart. If I believed that "due process" meant "due substance" when the Fourteenth Amendment was adopted,[23] I certainly would not feel free to abandon that meaning simply because nowadays we aspire to avoid words that mean the opposite of what they say.

PROFESSOR GLENDON

There is nothing I take sharp issue with in Professor Glendon's elegant statement, unless (for those familiar with *Young Franken-stein*) it is her failure to work in the Feldman-Wilder "Walk this way" routine. She makes the point that it is difficult to maintain and apply a coherent theory of statutory interpretation when dealing with statutes that are themselves incoherent—the "hast-ily cobbled compromises" of modern regulatory legislation, as opposed to "carefully drafted codes." That is unquestionably true. I would add, however, that what has been rendered more difficult has also been rendered more important. The more epi-sodic and oblivious of adjacent law modern legislation becomes,

---

Form Method in Constitutional Interpretation, 108 Harv. L. Rev. 1221, 1297 n.247 (1995).

[23] Of course I do not believe it. The only pre–Fourteenth Amendment au-thority the law-review article cites to prove that our ancestors favored oxymo-ron more than we do proves precisely the opposite—namely, the following statement in *Murray's Lessee* v. *Hoboken Land & Improvement Co.*, an 1855 case involving the constitutionality of a *procedure* whereby property was seized, without trial, to satisfy a debt allegedly owed to the government: "The [Due Process Clause] is a restraint on the legislative as well as on the executive and judicial powers of the government, and cannot be so construed as to leave congress free to make *any process 'due process of law,'* by its mere will." 59 U.S. (18 How.) 272, 276 (emphasis added). As far as I am aware, *Dred Scott* was the first and only pre–Fourteenth Amendment decision of the Supreme Court to employ substantive due process—and one can hardly argue that the reasoning of *that* case was part of America's accepted understanding.

the more crucial is the judicial function of making sense out of the whole, which can be achieved in principled fashion only through the application of legitimate interpretive techniques.

I will not quarrel with Professor Glendon over whether tyranny by the majority or tyranny by the powerful few is the more likely outcome of the theories of constitutional interpretation that now prevail. She thinks the latter. I think the latter in the short term (we are there now); but ultimately the former. Perhaps I overestimate the democratic vigor of our institutions. Or perhaps, because I am usually addressing my remarks to the powerful few themselves (those who belong to, or are in training for, the legal elite), I am biased in favor of majority control as the likely outcome, because that is the only thing that will strike fear into their hearts. In any event, neither outcome is a desirable one.

PROFESSOR DWORKIN

I agree with the distinction that Professor Dworkin draws in part 1 of his Comment, between what he calls "semantic intention" and the concrete expectations of lawgivers. It is indeed the former rather than the latter that I follow. I would prefer the term "import" to "semantic intention"—because that puts the focus where I believe it should be, upon what the text would reasonably be understood to mean, rather than upon what it was intended to mean. Ultimately, of course, those two concepts chase one another back and forth to some extent, since the import of language depends upon its context, which includes the occasion for, and hence the evident purpose of, its utterance. But so far Professor Dworkin and I are in accord: we both follow "semantic intention."

Professor Dworkin goes on to say, however, that I am not true to this calling, as is demonstrated, he believes, by my conviction that the Eighth Amendment does not forbid capital punishment. I am wrong in this, he says, because "the semantic-originalist . . .

must choose between two clarifying translations," the first of which "supposes that the framers intended to say, by using the words 'cruel and unusual,' that punishments generally thought cruel at the time they spoke were to be prohibited—that is, that they would have expressed themselves more clearly if they had used the phrase 'punishments widely regarded as cruel and unusual at the date of this enactment' in place of the misleading language they actually used," and the second of which "supposes that they intended to lay down an abstract principle forbidding whatever punishments are in fact cruel and unusual." This seems to me a false dichotomy, the first part of which caricatures my sort of originalism, much as Professor Tribe did—as a narrow and hidebound methodology that ascribes to the Constitution a listing of rights "in highly particularistic, rule-like terms." In fact, however, I, no less than Professor Dworkin, believe that the Eighth Amendment is no mere "concrete and dated rule" but rather an abstract principle. If I did not hold this belief, I would not be able to apply the Eighth Amendment (as I assuredly do) to all sorts of tortures quite unknown at the time the Eighth Amendment was adopted. What it abstracts, however, is not a moral principle of "cruelty" that philosophers can play with in the future, but rather the existing society's assessment of what is cruel. It means not (as Professor Dworkin would have it) "whatever may be considered cruel from one generation to the next," but "what we consider cruel today"; otherwise, it would be no protection against the moral perceptions of a future, more brutal, generation. It is, in other words, rooted in the moral perceptions *of the time*.

On this analysis, it is entirely clear that capital punishment, which was widely in use in 1791, does not violate the abstract moral principle of the Eighth Amendment. Professor Dworkin is therefore close to correct in saying that the *textual* evidence I cite for the constitutionality of capital punishment (namely, the specific mention of it in several portions of the Bill of Rights) ought to be "irrelevant" to me. To be entirely correct, he should have said "superfluous." Surely the same point *can* be proved by textual evidence, even though (as far as my philosophy is concerned) it need not be. I adduced the textual evidence only to demonstrate that thoroughgoing constitutional evolutionists will be no more deterred by text than by theory.

Professor Dworkin nonetheless takes on my textual point and seeks to prove it wrong. He asserts that making provision for the death penalty in the Constitution does not establish that it was not regarded as "cruel" under the Eighth Amendment, just as making provision for mink-hunting licenses in a statute which forbids the hunting of "endangered species" does not establish that minks can never acquire the protected status of an "endangered species." To begin with, I am not as clear as he is that such a fanciful statute—which simply forbids the hunting of "endangered species" without conferring authority upon some agency to define what species are endangered from time to time—would be interpreted to have a changing content; or, if it were so interpreted, that minks, for which hunting licenses are authorized, can come within that changing content. But if the example does suggest those consequences, it is only because the term "endangered species," unlike the term "cruel punishments," clearly connotes a category that changes from decade to decade. Animal populations, we will all agree, ebb and flow, and hence it is plausible to believe that minks, even though "unendangered" and marked for hunting when the statute was passed, might come under "endangered species" protection in the future. Unlike animal populations, however, "moral principles," most of us think, are permanent. The Americans of 1791 surely thought that what was cruel was cruel, regardless of what a more brutal future generation might think about it. They were embedding in the Bill of Rights *their* moral values, for otherwise all its general and abstract guarantees could be brought to nought. Thus, provision for the death penalty in a Constitution that sets forth the moral principle of "no cruel punishments" is conclusive evidence that the death penalty is not (in the moral view of the Constitution) cruel.

Professor Dworkin asserts that the three arguments I have made against an evolutionary meaning of the Bill of Rights do not comport with my methodology of "semantic intent." I disagree. The first of them, argument from the unquestionably "time-dated" character of the concrete provisions to the conclusion that the more abstract provisions are time-dated as well, is not, as Professor Dworkin asserts, a "speculation[ ] about the expectations of [their] authors," but is rather a quite routine attempt to divine import ("semantic intent") from *context*. In fact, it is nothing more than an application of the canon of construction *noscitur ex sociis*, which I discussed in my main essay. The second argument also rests upon context—a context which shows that the purpose of the document in question is to guarantee certain rights, which in turn leads to the conclusion that the passage of time cannot reasonably be thought to alter the content of those rights. And the third, the argument that the repository of ultimate responsibility for determining the content of the rights (the judiciary) is a most unlikely barometer of evolving national morality but a traditional interpreter of "time-dated" laws, rests upon context as well—assuming (as a given) that judicial review is implicit in the structure of the Constitution. Of course if, as both Professor Dworkin and Professor Tribe seem to suggest, it is not a given that the Bill of Rights is to be enforced against the legislature by the courts, then my argument ceases to have force as a justification for my mode of interpretation but becomes an argument directed to the overall inconsistency of the evolutionists: Why, given what they believe the Bill of Rights is, would they want judges to be its ultimate interpreters?

As for Professor Dworkin's point that the First Amendment cannot possibly be "time-dated" because "[t]here *was* no generally accepted understanding of the right of free speech": On the main points, I think, there was. But even if not, it is infinitely more reasonable to interpret a document as leaving some of the uncertainties of the current state of the law to be worked out in practice and in litigation (statutes do this all the time) than to interpret it as enacting, and making judicially enforceable, an indeterminate moral concept of "freedom of speech." It makes a lot of sense to guarantee to a society that "the freedom of speech you now enjoy (*whatever* that consists of) will never be diminished by the federal government"; it makes very little sense to guarantee that "the federal government will respect the moral principle of freedom of speech, which may entitle you to more, or less, freedom of speech than you now legally enjoy."

Professor Dworkin also criticizes my discussion of the Fourteenth Amendment—in the course of which he confuses, I think, two issues. First, he quotes my statement that the Equal Protection Clause "did not, when it was adopted, and hence did not in 1920, guarantee equal access to the ballot but permitted distinctions on the basis not only of age but of property and sex." He then asks, "Why is he so sure that the Equal Protection Clause did not always forbid discrimination on grounds of age, property, or sex (or, for that matter, sexual orientation)? . . . If we look at the text . . ., we see no distinction . . . ." In fact, however, as far as access to the ballot goes (which was the subject of my quoted remark), the text of the Fourteenth Amendment is very clear that equal protection does not mean equal access on the basis of (at least) age and sex. Section 2 of the amendment provides for reduction of representation in Congress if a state excludes from the ballot "any of the male inhabitants of such State, being twenty-one years of age." But as for the application of the Equal Protection Clause *generally* (which is what Professor Dworkin proceeds to address), he quite entirely mistakes my position. I certainly do not assert that it permits discrimination on the basis of age, property, sex, "sexual orientation," or for that matter even blue eyes and nose rings. Denial of equal protection on *all* of these grounds is prohibited—but that still leaves open the question of what *constitutes* a denial of equal protection. Is it a denial of equal protection on the basis of sex to have segregated toilets in public buildings, or to exclude women from combat? I have no idea how Professor Dworkin goes about

148

answering such a question. I answer it on the basis of the "time-dated" meaning of equal protection in 1868. Unisex toilets and women assault troops may be ideas whose time has come, and the people are certainly free to require them by legislation; but refusing to do so does not violate the Fourteenth Amendment, because that is not what "equal protection of the laws" ever meant.

Finally, Professor Dworkin dismisses my fears that, in the long run, the "moral reading" of the Constitution will lead to a reduction of the rights of individuals. "History disagrees," he says, since "the people seem content not only with the moral reading but with its individualist implications." Well, there is not really much history to go on. As I have observed, evolutionary constitutional jurisprudence has held sway in the courts for only forty years or so, and recognition by the people that the Constitution means whatever it ought to mean is even more recent. To be sure, there are still notable victories in the Supreme Court for "individual rights," but has Professor Dworkin not observed that, increasingly, the "individual rights" favored by the courts tend to be the same "individual rights" favored by popular majoritarian legislation? Women's rights, for example; racial minority rights; homosexual rights; abortion rights; rights against political favoritism? The glorious days of the Warren Court, when the *judges* knew that the Constitution means whatever it ought to, but the *people* had not yet caught on to the new game (and selected their judges accordingly), are gone forever. Those were the days in which genuinely *unpopular* new minority rights could be created—notably, rights of criminal defendants and prisoners. That era of public naiveté is past, and for individual rights disfavored by the majority I think there are hard times ahead.

☆ *Contributors* ☆

RONALD DWORKIN is Professor of Law at New York University and Professor of Jurisprudence at Oxford University. He is author of *Taking Rights Seriously*, *A Matter of Principle*, *Law's Empire*, *Philosophical Issues in Senile Dementia*, *A Bill of Rights for Britain*, and *Life's Dominion*. He received a B.A. at both Harvard College and Oxford University, and then his L.L.B. from Harvard Law School.

MARY ANN GLENDON is the Learned Hand Professor of Law at Harvard University. She is author of *A Nation under Lawyers*, *The New Family and the New Property*, *Abortion and Divorce in Western Law*, *The Transformation of Family Laws*, and *Rights Talk*. She graduated from the University of Chicago and received her doctorate from the Universities of Chicago and Louvain.

AMY GUTMANN is Laurance S. Rockefeller Professor of Politics and Dean of the Faculty at Princeton University. Among her publications are *Democratic Education*, *Democracy and Disagreement* (with Dennis Thompson), and *Color Conscious: The Political Morality of Race* (with K. Anthony Appiah). She graduated from Harvard-Radcliffe College and received her M.Sc. from the London School of Economics and her Ph.D. from Harvard.

ANTONIN SCALIA has been an Associate Justice of the United States Supreme Court since 1986. Prior to that time he served on the U.S. Court of Appeals for the District of Columbia, and taught at the University of Virginia and the University of Chicago. He graduated from Georgetown University and received his LL.B. from Harvard University.

LAURENCE TRIBE is Ralph S. Tyler, Jr. Professor of Constitutional Law at Harvard Law School. He is author of *On Reading the Constitution*, *Abortion: The Clash of Absolutes*, *American Constitutional Law*, *God Save This Honorable Court: How the Choice of Supreme Court Justices Shapes Our History*, and *Constitutional Choices*. He graduated from Harvard College and received his J.D. at Harvard Law School.

151

GORDON WOOD is Professor of American History at Brown University. He is author of *The Creation of the American Republic, 1776–1787*; editor of *Rising Glory of America, 1760–1820*; and coauthor of *The Great Republic*. He graduated from Tufts University and received his A.M. and Ph.D. at Harvard University.

☆ *Index* ☆